WinRT Revealed

Michael Mayberry

Apress®

WinRT Revealed

ISBN-13 (pbk): 978-1-4302-4584-1

ISBN-13 (electronic): 978-1-4302-4585-8

President and Publisher: Paul Manning
Lead Editor: James Markham
Technical Reviewer: Jeff Sanders
Editorial Board: Steve Anglin, Ewan Buckingham, Gary Cornell, Louise Corrigan, Morgan Ertel, Jonathan Gennick, Jonathan Hassell, Robert Hutchinson, Michelle Lowman, James Markham, Matthew Moodie, Jeff Olson, Jeffrey Pepper, Douglas Pundick, Ben Renow-Clarke, Dominic Shakeshaft, Gwenan Spearing, Matt Wade, Tom Welsh
Coordinating Editor: Debra Kelly
Copy Editor: William McManus
Compositor: SPi Global
Indexer: SPi Global
Artist: SPi Global
Cover Designer: Anna Ishchenko

Distributed to the book trade worldwide by Springer Science+Business Media New York, 233 Spring Street, 6th Floor, New York, NY 10013. Phone 1-800-SPRINGER, fax (201) 348-4505, e-mail `orders-ny@springer-sbm.com`, or visit `www.springeronline.com`.

For information on translations, please e-mail `rights@apress.com`, or visit `www.apress.com`.

Apress and friends of ED books may be purchased in bulk for academic, corporate, or promotional use. eBook versions and licenses are also available for most titles. For more information, reference our Special Bulk Sales–eBook Licensing web page at `www.apress.com/bulk-sales`.

To Grandpa Hyde, thanks for buying my first computer.

Contents at a Glance

Contents

About the Author

Michael Mayberry has been developing software with Microsoft technologies for more than 13 years. Over those years he has consistently adopted new solutions and tools to solve increasingly larger problems.

Michael currently serves as a software architect for a large nonprofit organization in the Dallas-Fort Worth area. He has become an expert in integration, providing solutions that allow new software to interact with existing systems. His experiences range from content management systems to data warehouses to CRM systems.

Michael has always valued team building and sharing his knowledge with others. Recently, he expanded his focus to include writing and reviewing. He has been a technical reviewer for many projects and coauthored one other book.

When he is not working, Michael enjoys spending time with his beautiful wife and four children.

For questions and comments, contact Michael at `michaelmayberry@hotmail.com`.

About the Technical Reviewer

Jeff Sanders is a published author, technical editor, and accomplished technologist. He is currently employed with Avanade in the capacity of a group manager/senior architect.

Jeff has years of professional experience in the field of IT and strategic business consulting, leading both sales and delivery efforts. He regularly contributes to certification and product roadmap development with Microsoft and speaks publicly on Microsoft enterprise technologies. With his roots in software development, Jeff's areas of expertise include collaboration and content management solutions, operational intelligence, digital marketing, distributed component-based application architectures, object-oriented analysis and design, and enterprise integration patterns and designs.

Jeff is also the CTO of DynamicShift, a client-focused organization specializing in Microsoft technologies, specifically Office365/BPOS, SharePoint Server, StreamInsight, Windows Azure, AppFabric, Business Activity Monitoring, BizTalk Server, and .NET. He is a Microsoft Certified Trainer, and he leads DynamicShift in both training and consulting efforts.

He enjoys non-work-related travel and spending time with his wife and daughter, and he wishes he had more time for both.

Jeff may be reached at `jeff.sanders@dynamicshift.com`.

Acknowledgments

I first bow my head in thanks to Jesus Christ for giving meaning to life and providing the way for us to see the love God has for us all. Thank you for the blessings that make a project like this even possible.

I thank my wife, Camille. She makes our home a great place to work, write, and play. Thank you for your encouragement and support.

Thank you to everyone at Apress who worked so hard to make this project happen so quickly. I truly appreciate your effort in making this book possible.

Introduction

Windows 8 provides a new and exciting platform for developers. This coming version of Windows promises to run on new hardware, such as tablets, as well as existing laptops and desktops. Microsoft has developed a new layer for accessing and leveraging system resources, including the operating system services. The new Windows Runtime (WinRT) is this layer.

Who Is This Book For?

This book is an introduction to WinRT. With the Windows Runtime being so new, developers of all experience ranges can benefit from this introduction. This book demonstrates how to build Windows 8 Metro style apps, specifically focusing on WinRT.

How This Book Is Structured

There are only four chapters in this book, but each one is packed with information designed to get developers familiar with WinRT.

This short book begins with an overview of WinRT in the first chapter, which explains what WinRT is and answers common questions developers have about the Windows Runtime.

The following chapter demonstrates coding with WinRT. The first examples start simple and show how WinRT components are built.

The final two chapters focus on building Metro style apps. The developer builds apps that use WinRT components to interface with the user. They also extend their app to interact with other apps.

Downloading the Code

The code for the examples shown in this book is available on the Apress web site, `www.apress.com`. A link can be found on the book's information page under the Source Code/Downloads tab. This tab is located underneath the Related Titles section of the page.

CHAPTER 1

Introducing WinRT

The fact that you are reading this means you know that Windows 8 is coming, and that this is a big deal. Microsoft Windows is changing, and developers need to be ready. While Windows will continue to provide an environment for the current methods of development, Microsoft is introducing a new environment. This one is focused on apps rather than on programs, and on mobile devices with touch interfaces rather than on desktops and laptops.

With these changes in design and approach to development, Microsoft has also introduced a new way for software to access system resources. The OS will be running on new types of devices with new ways for the user to interact with the software. The industry's entire approach to developing consumer-based software is changing. Microsoft recognized the need for a different way to expose the OS functionality to developers. Windows 8 needs a new layer for Metro apps. This layer is the Windows Runtime, or WinRT.

To introduce WinRT, the following topics will be addressed in this chapter:

- What WinRT is
- What WinRT is not
- How WinRT works
- WinRT and the user experience
- Asynchronous by nature
- The WinRT API

What Is WinRT?

Search the Internet for "WinRT" and you will find that developers all over the Web are asking this very question. Many blogs and websites have attempted to answer this question. Several do a great job, but it can get confusing as answers begin to contradict each other. Is WinRT based on COM? Is WinRT just .NET? Does WinRT kill Silverlight? This book addresses the primary question, "What is WinRT?" In doing so, it answers these other questions as well. The purpose of this book is to help developers understand WinRT and how they leverage it for their development. How big is the "learning curve" for this thing? It is not as difficult as you may think. You will see some examples of coding with WinRT and can follow along yourself with the downloadable sample code. When you finish this book, WinRT will no longer be a mystery.

MSDN describes WinRT as "a straightforward set of APIs used to build Metro style apps." It is a new framework or programming model for building Metro software. This is how Windows 8 exposes the system services to the apps installed and running on the machine. This includes the display. UI development uses Extensible Application Markup Language (XAML) components, which are part of WinRT. These APIs are available to developers in many supported languages:

- C#
- Visual Basic

- C++
- JavaScript

Figure 1-1 was shown at the 2011 Build conference, when Microsoft introduced Windows 8 development. The WinRT APIs are consumed directly from the various languages used to write Metro style apps. There are other layers that make this work, but the developer does not need to worry about them. Those layers are handled by Visual Studio or Windows 8. What those layers are and how they make this all work is discussed a little later in the chapter. From the perspective of writing code, Figure 1-1 shows how the multiple supported languages can directly interact with WinRT components.

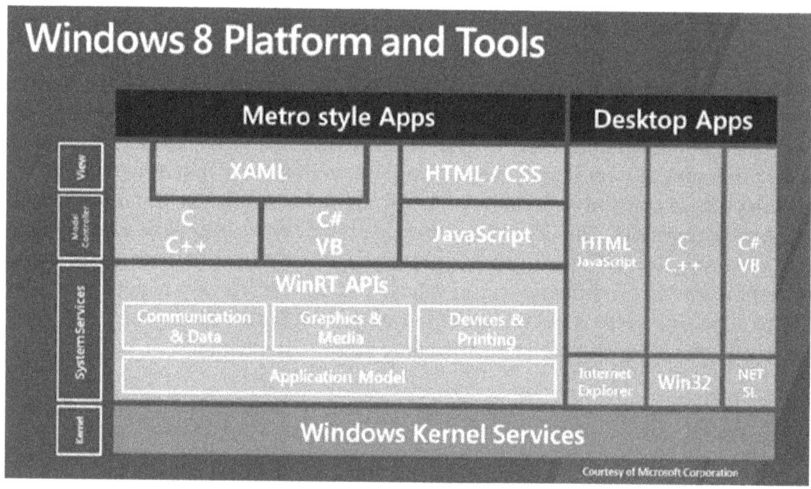

Figure 1-1. *Windows 8 Platform and Tools diagram*

■ **Tip** The Windows 8 Platform and Tools diagram has been widely discussed on the Internet. Many developers feel it lacks certain details as an architectural diagram. For more discussion on this diagram, visit http://dougseven.com/2011/09/15/a-bad-picture-is-worth-a-thousand-long-discussions.

As you can see in the diagram, all Metro style apps rely on WinRT for access to the system resources. This includes everything from interfaces to display, devices to storage. The reliance upon WinRT is direct. Developers in all languages can call WinRT components directly in a seamless manner. Developers will need to understand WinRT to successfully design and build Metro apps for Windows 8.

What WinRT Is Not

For general clarification, it may be helpful to provide an up-front explanation of what WinRT is not:

> *WinRT is not .NET (nor a subset thereof):* The new Windows Runtime is not a subset of anything. It is a new framework and the sole provider of all Windows system services to Metro style apps. It is not a part of .NET, but it is used by the .NET languages, as well as the other supported languages.

WinRT is not cross-platform: Windows uses the Windows Runtime to expose system services. When your app uses the WinRT APIs, it does so to access those Windows services. Therefore, WinRT is not used in any other context. It is used in Windows apps for Windows devices.

WinRT is not based on Win32: WinRT replaces Win32 for Metro development. This is a new execution layer, and the programming model is very different from Win32. Don't worry, though, because Win32 is still included in Windows 8. Thus, legacy software will continue to work.

■ **Note** WinRT is written in C++ and has been designed as object-oriented. The support of reflection provides efficiency to dynamic languages such as JavaScript.

How Does WinRT Work?

To develop Windows 8 apps, you must move away from Win32. However, everything developed prior to now has been built on Win32. Developers have been investing in Windows Forms, Windows Presentation Foundation (WPF), and Silverlight, which are all based on Win32. Now developers have to change to WinRT? Yet, Microsoft says they can still use the skills they have learned? How is this possible? This section provides the answers.

Projections

The WinRT APIs are native, meaning they are written in C++ and compiled to binaries run against the core Windows services. There is no Common Language Runtime (CLR) or other type of interpreter in the middle. In the past, using native components has not been a pleasant experience for developers. Heavy use of COM was required to get to native components. With WinRT, Microsoft has changed this.

Microsoft supports multiple languages for app development in Windows 8. Microsoft also wanted to make accessing the core Windows services as simple as possible. For this purpose, Microsoft has provided language *projections*.

Projections expose a WinRT component to a particular language in a way that fits that language. The syntax for accessing a WinRT component looks just like the syntax for accessing any other component written in that same language. For example, writing a C# app uses C# syntax to access WinRT components:

```
var picker = new Windows.Storage.Pickers.FileOpenPicker();
picker.FileTypeFilter.Add(".jpg");
await picker.PickSingleFileAsync();
```

Writing a JavaScript app uses JavaScript syntax to access WinRT components:

```
var picker = new Windows.Storage.Pickers.FileOpenPicker;
picker.fileTypeFilter.append(".jpg");
picker.pickSingleFileAsync().then();
```

Even native apps use projections, and working with WinRT components feels just like working with any other C++ API:

```
auto picker = ref Windows::Storage::Pickers::FileOpenPicker();
picker->FileTypeFilter->Append(".jpg");
auto asyncObj = picker->PickSingleFileAsync();
asyncObj->Start();
```

Microsoft has provided the mapping to make this work. This allows developers to consume WinRT components in a natural way.

This level of accessibility remains true as you design and develop your own components based on WinRT. These custom components can be consumed in any of the supported languages.

Windows Metadata

By nature, native components do not include metadata in their files. Microsoft, however, needed metadata to make WinRT's design work. Enter Windows Metadata (WinMD). Every WinRT component has a WinMD file associated with it. This file contains all of the information needed by the operating system and other software to access this component. Microsoft uses the same format (ECMA-335) for this new type of file that it uses in the .NET framework.

■ **Note** When you build a Windows Runtime component, Visual Studio will generate a .winmd file that is created and registered on the machine. WinRT component information is entered into the Windows Registry when it is installed on the machine.

When these WinRT components are accessed by software of different languages, the Windows Metadata is what makes all of this work. First, Visual Studio uses the metadata to populate IntelliSense to enhance the development experience and provide the necessary details during design time. Second, the different languages access the WinMD file for the information they need to bind the component at the appropriate time.

■ **Note** The WinMD files can be found in the Windows\System32\WinMetaData folder. They are all stored here by Windows 8. These files can be inspected using the ILDASM tool.

Support Languages and WinMD

The WinMD files allow the supported languages to use the WinRT components. This involves projection, as described earlier, but how exactly does this work? WinRT works with native code, the CLR, and dynamic code. Figure 1-2 depicts how each language accesses the Windows Metadata.

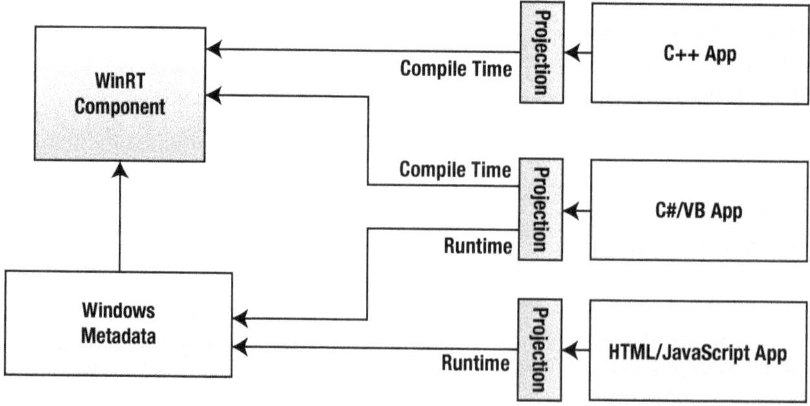

Figure 1-2. *How Windows Metadata is accessed from apps*

When building Metro style apps in C++, the compiler accesses Windows Metadata-based projections and builds the necessary binaries as part of the app. The metadata is not accessed again during runtime. The app has all of the information it needs for successful execution.

When building Metro style apps in C# or Visual Basic, the CLR accesses the Windows Metadata at compile time. Where .NET apps differ from native apps is in the fact that .NET apps also access the metadata at runtime. Microsoft claims these calls are negligible and will not affect performance.

JavaScript is a dynamic language, so everything is compiled and bound at runtime. The Chakra engine uses the Windows Metadata during this process, making the installed WinRT components available to the Metro style apps written in JavaScript.

Windows Metadata ensures that all WinRT components are accessible to all apps running in Windows 8, regardless of the language in which they were written. This accessibility is extended into design time as developers build their apps using these WinRT components.

■ **Note** Windows 8 includes a runtime broker service that ensures that apps have the proper permissions to access resources. Many calls will run directly against the Windows Kernel Services, but some, such as file pickers, will be caught by the broker service and prompt the user for permission.

Building the User Experience

When it comes to developing the user experience for Windows 8 (see Figure 1-3), developers have two choices: XAML or HTML5. XAML is used by .NET and C++ developers, while HTML5 pairs with JavaScript.

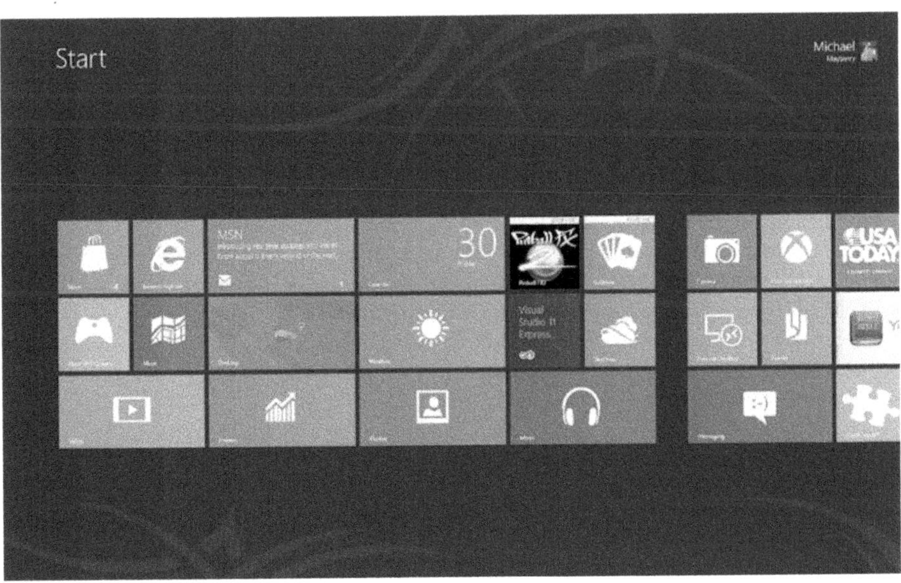

Figure 1-3. *Windows 8 Start screen*

XAML

XAML controls are actually part of WinRT. Windows Forms and WPF controls are based on Win32, so they will not run in the Metro space. WinRT includes all new controls. Developers using C++ will now use XAML to build the UI for apps. Silverlight and WPF developers will carry forward their knowledge into a familiar design experience.

XAML is a nice markup language for developing the UI for an application. Many developers have certainly found themselves building the UI by writing the XAML by hand. Most developers prefer tools, and Microsoft delivers. Expression Blend has been around for many years as a designer tool for building the UI and generating the XAML for further development. Designers and developers will continue to have access to Blend for Windows 8 Metro development. The Visual Studio 11 Beta download includes the next version of Blend for this purpose.

HTML5

Windows 8 fully supports using HTML5/CSS3 for the presentation layer of your apps. That is an interesting thought. Maybe you are thinking of Windows 8 running on a tablet, similar to an iPad, and the thought of HTML rendering the UI is not a big deal. But Windows 8 runs on laptops and PCs as well. The thought of an HTML UI for a "desktop" experience is new and interesting. This is not web development. This is PC development.

Developers with HTML and CSS3 skills can bring what they already know to Windows app development. JavaScript directly uses WinRT, so no new syntax or language needs to be introduced. To make the jump to the Metro design a bit easier, Microsoft offers JavaScript and CSS for use in your projects.

WinRT apps using HTML will not run in a browser. They are meant for the Windows 8 experience only. While that is somewhat of a shift in thought, it can also be a freeing concept. The idea of using HTML and CSS3 together with JavaScript to build a clean and fast app without struggling against the issues introduced by the browser environment is a nice thought indeed.

Blend for HTML

Microsoft delivers the power of Expression Blend to the world of HTML. If you have used Blend in the past, you understand that this is no small deal. If you have not used Blend, you may be thinking you do not need another design editor. In fact, you may have long ago abandoned WYSIWYG editors for HTML and manually code your UI by hand. Believe this, Blend is not just an HTML editor.

Blend for HTML allows you to work with your application UI written in HTML together with your JavaScript controls and CSS styles. The design surface within Blend actually runs your JavaScript code. Even if you create some of the UI elements in code, your UI will be rendered properly on the screen.

You can even work with your app with an interactive mode. This allows you to "use" your app and bring the UI to the state you need to access.

Asynchronous by Nature

It seems users' tolerance for slower performance is greatly affected by the hardware on which the software is running. For large PCs, having to wait a bit for things to work seems to be tolerable to users. On a tablet, however, waiting becomes much more annoying. We are quick to uninstall apps with too much lag time. Having to wait more than a few seconds for apps on our smartphones to respond tempts us to buy new devices altogether. Microsoft understands this and has designed Windows Runtime with performance in mind. Microsoft set the threshold very low. Any call into WinRT that takes longer than 50ms is asynchronous by default. That is 1/20th of a second. Anything that takes longer than that runs asynchronously.

While Silverlight developers may be familiar with asynchronous design, the typical desktop programmer may not be. In the world of Windows 8, synchronous programming just will not work. The Metro style is not only a look, but a certain feel as well. Microsoft describes it as "fast and fluid." Expectations are high.

WinRT ensures that apps remain responsive to the user at all times. In the past, synchronous programming was preferred because it was so much simpler. Writing async code meant more complexity in design and in programming. Now, however, languages like C# and VB support the `await/async` pattern. C++ uses lambdas; JavaScript uses promises and `then()`. Asynchronous programming is made simple. There is still a shift in one's mindset that must occur, but the syntax and process handling has been simplified.

■ **Note** Multithreading in WinRT is still available in the System.Threading namespace. The expectation, however, is that most developers will use the asynchronous methods discussed here because they will be sufficient for most UI and application needs.

Despite what you may be thinking, forcing developers into the asynchronous model is a good thing. You will explore this in more detail in later chapters.

THE CONSUMER MINDSET

Developers are content providers. You build the apps and websites that consumers desire to use. Developing that content requires many specialized tools and functionality. Pure consumers are not like developers. The needs they have from their machines are much simpler. Think of the machine you would build for yourself versus the machine you would build for your grandparents or for your neighbor who simply wants to surf the Internet a bit and check e-mail. Your consumer friends and family do not need much power. Their PCs are not required to work hard, and most of the functionality from whatever operating system they use remains unused.

Devices like tablets and smartphones take advantage of this difference. Check the specs of your development machine against those of the iPad. In all likelihood, the machine you once used that is now sitting in the corner has more processing power than the vastly popular iPad. However, the consumer simply does not care. Websites load quickly, e-mail appears smoothly, and the touch interface blows everything else out of the proverbial water.

It is with this understanding that Microsoft provides the development environment for consumer apps. The full power of Windows Core Services is not needed for consumer apps. In fact, successful apps require streamlining their foundation to maintain performance and usability over time. The desktop experience is still available, and Windows 8 will run on powerful machines. Content providers can still take advantage of Windows 8, but the Metro experience is designed for consumers.

When designing apps for Windows 8, you must keep this in mind as well. You will build apps for consumers when using WinRT. Otherwise, you are most likely building software for providers or enterprise users. Metro style development is not aimed at those scenarios. WinRT exposes only the services needed for a great consumer experience.

The WinRT API

Much of the functionality available in WinRT was previously available in .NET. For the Metro context, Microsoft moved that functionality into WinRT. The functionality has not actually been removed from .NET. For contexts outside of Metro development, the full range of .NET is available.

Some .NET developers will not agree with this move. The way they have been doing something for the past 10 years is now different. However, one benefit is that it can now be done from other languages outside of .NET. This is an attractive feature for Microsoft to offer.

■ **Note** WinRT applications run in a sandbox. Each app is isolated and is only allowed to access what WinRT allows. With this in mind, many of the changes Microsoft introduced in WinRT make sense.

So what is in WinRT? What exactly does it expose? Take a look at the top namespaces in the WinRT API:

Windows.ApplicationModel

Windows.Data

Windows.Devices

Windows.Foundation

Windows.Globalization

Windows.Graphics

Windows.Management

Windows.Media

Windows.Networking

Windows.Security

Windows.Storage

Windows.System

Windows.UI

Windows.Web

The list is not long, but can you see the focus on the user experience here? WinRT provides exposure to the system services needed in consumer-based app development.

■ **Tip** For more information regarding the full WinRT API, visit http://msdn.microsoft.com/en-us/library/windows/apps/br211377.aspx.

Not everything available in .NET is available in WinRT. This may be why some developers think of WinRT as a subset of .NET. That is not actually the case. WinRT is separate from .NET. However, .NET already included functionality to access system resources. Microsoft moved this functionality to the new Windows Runtime for Metro development.

The functionality that was not moved is still mostly accessible in .NET. Metro development works similar to a .NET profile, exposing only those namespaces that are allowed and supported. This is similar to how Silverlight uses a specific .NET profile and only exposes what is allowed and supported for that context.

Summary

Windows 8 is designed with the consumer in mind. WinRT provides the access to the system resources to build great consumer-focused Metro apps. First-class support is given to .NET, HTML/JavaScript, and C++ for app development.

WinRT exposes the system resources in a way that is natural for the developer in their language of choice.

Now it is time to get into some code. The rest of the chapters in this book focus on developing with WinRT, using example code to show how things work.

Get out your Windows 8 development machine, or at least start up Visual Studio 11 Beta, and get ready to dive into WinRT.

CHAPTER 2

Building WinRT Components

Reading about WinRT can be very helpful. Watching online videos or attending conferences to learn about WinRT can also be helpful. However, there is nothing like working through code yourself to learn how it works and figure out how to make it fit your needs.

In this chapter you will

- Build a simple WinRT component using C#
- Consume your simple WinRT component in your JavaScript app

Note The projects in this book were written using Visual Studio 11 Beta on a laptop with Windows 8 Consumer Preview installed. All apps were tested by running them directly on the laptop, when possible. You may also choose to run your apps in the emulator included in Visual Studio 11 Beta.

First, the Ground Rules

In this chapter, you will build a WinRT component using Visual C#. When using .NET to build WinRT components, there are four rules that must be followed:

1. API signatures must only use WinRT types.
2. Structs can only have public data fields.
3. All types must be sealed (except for XAML).
4. Only system-provided generic types are supported.

As discussed in Chapter 1, all WinRT components may be used by any of the supporting languages. This is not true for pure .NET components. So the preceding rules must be followed to develop a WinRT component using .NET. It is very surprising that there are only four of these rules. You will see how these rules apply in the sample code later in this chapter. However, WinRT type mapping needs some introduction.

Type Mapping

Remember, WinRT components are native. The types in .NET are not available to WinRT. Type mapping must occur to make this work. Table 2-1 contains the most common types.

Table 2-1. *WinRT to .NET Type Mapping*

.NET Framework	Windows Runtime
IEnumerable<T>	IIterable<T>
IEnumerator<T>	IIterator<T>
IList<T>	IVector<T>
IReadOnlyList<T>	IVectorView<T>
IDictionary<TKey, TValue>	IMap<K, V>
IReadOnlyDictionary<TKey, TValue>	IMapView<K, V>
IEnumerable	IBindableIterable
IList	IBindableVector

Most of the time, type mapping occurs automatically and the developer does not need to be concerned. However, when building a WinRT component and the return types can only be WinRT types, these type maps need to be considered.

Create a Simple JavaScript App

To demonstrate how WinRT components are built and used, you will create a simple JavaScript app that will consume a WinRT component written in Visual C#.

Create the Solution

You first need to create the project and solution.

1. Start Visual Studio 11 Beta on your Windows 8 development machine.
2. Create a new project and select the JavaScript Windows Metro style template, as shown in Figure 2-1.
3. Name the project **Chapter02_WinRT_Components** and choose a location on your machine.
4. Click OK.

Now the JavaScript project is created, along with the entire solution. While JavaScript apps are fascinating, they are not the focus of this book. So leave the JavaScript app alone for a bit.

Build a Simple WinRT Component

Now you will add a second project for the Visual C# WinRT component.

1. Right-click the solution and click Add ➤ New Project, as shown in Figure 2-2.

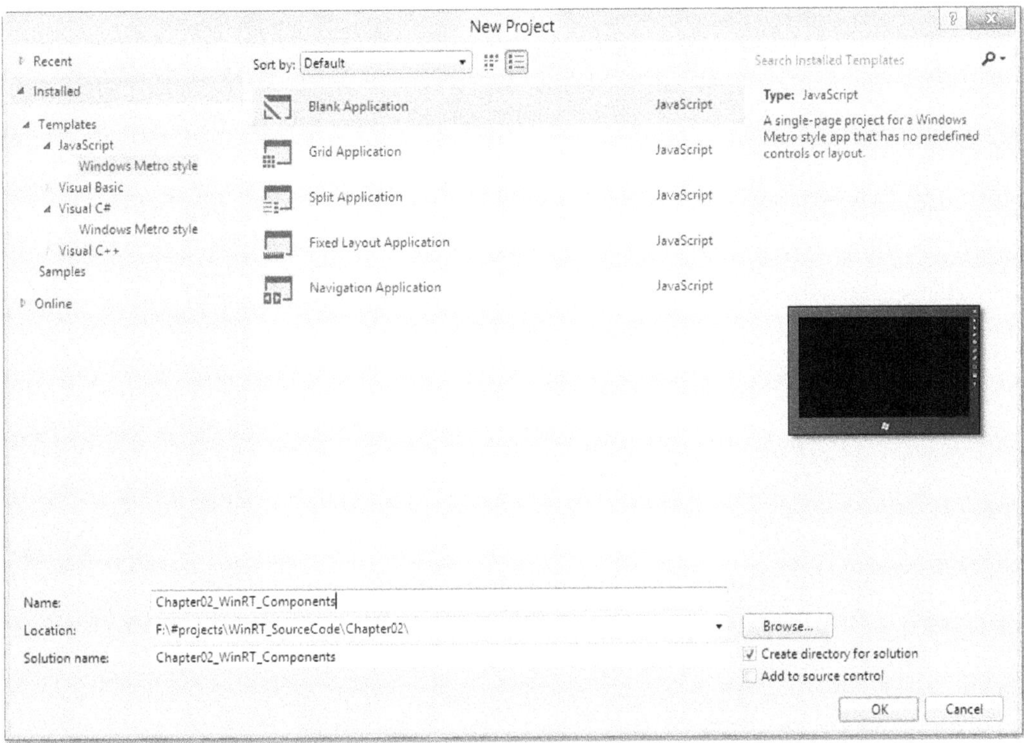

Figure 2-1. *Creating a new JavaScript Metro style project*

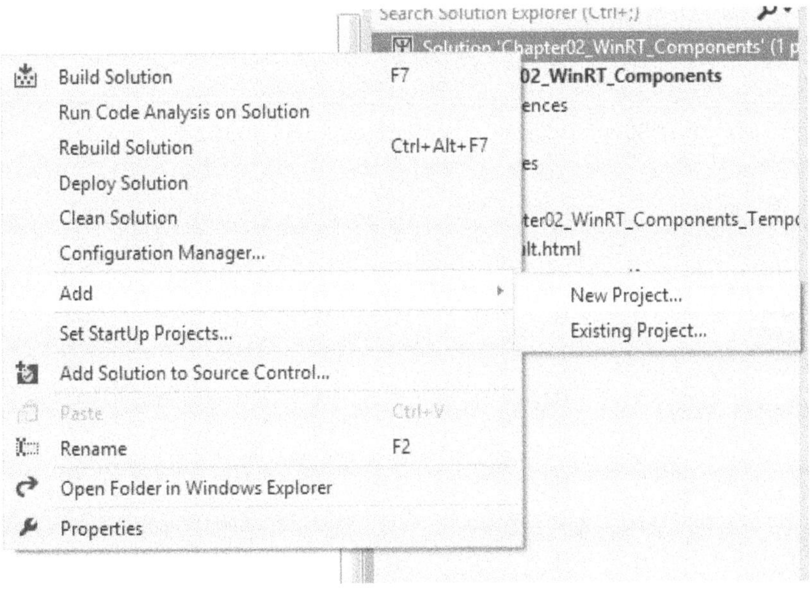

Figure 2-2. *Adding an additional project to the solution*

2. Select the Visual C# Class Library template and name the project **SimpleSource**. Click OK when your screen appears similar to Figure 2-3.

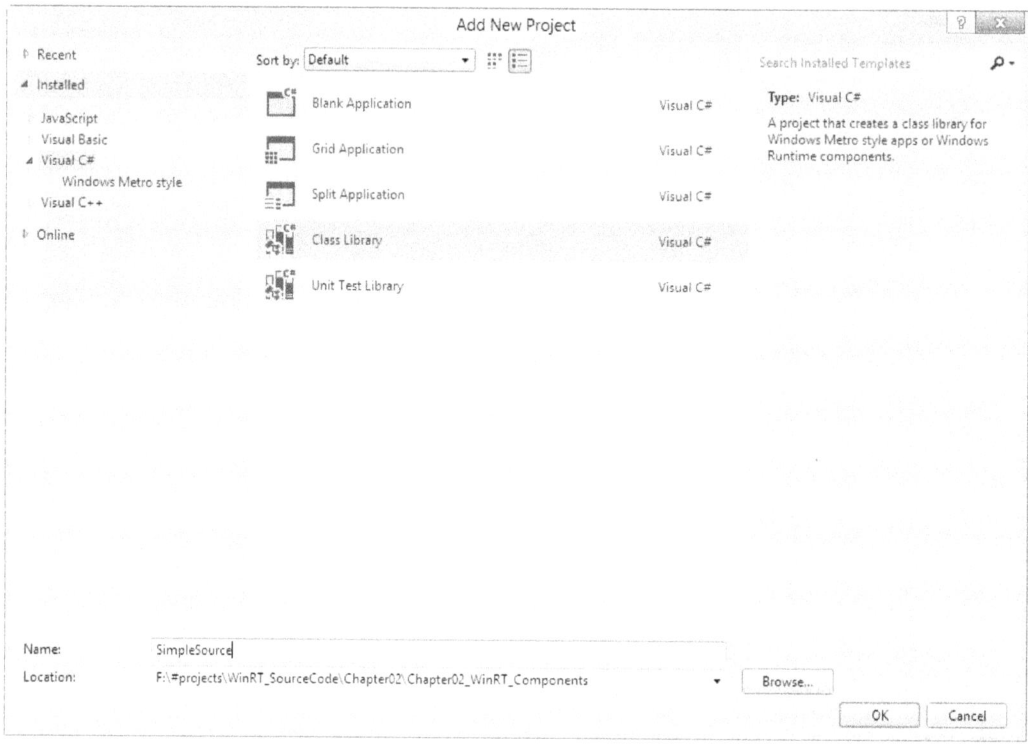

***Figure 2-3.** Adding a class library to the project for the WinRT component*

3. Add a class named **SimpleData** and enter the code from Listing 2-1.

Listing 2-1. SimpleData.cs

```
using System;
using System.Collections.Generic;
using System.Linq;
using System.Text;
using System.Threading.Tasks;

namespace SimpleSource
{
    public sealed class SimpleData
    {
       public string appTitle { get { return "WinRT Revealed Sample app"; }}
    }
}
```

This is an extremely simple class. The single property returns the title of the app as a string. Even in this very simple example, there are a couple of important things to notice:

> *No Windows namespaces:* The WinRT controls and components provided by Microsoft are all found in the Windows namespace. For this component, no Windows namespaces were used. This simply means that this component does not *consume* other WinRT components, but it still is one itself.
>
> *Public sealed class:* Every class must be a public sealed class to compile into a WinRT component.

The code is written and the project will build successfully. However, the output will be a .dll file. For WinRT components, you need a .winmd file. You need to change the output type to WinMD File to accomplish this.

4. Right-click the SimpleSource project and click Properties. Select WinMD File from the Output type drop-down list, as shown in Figure 2-4.

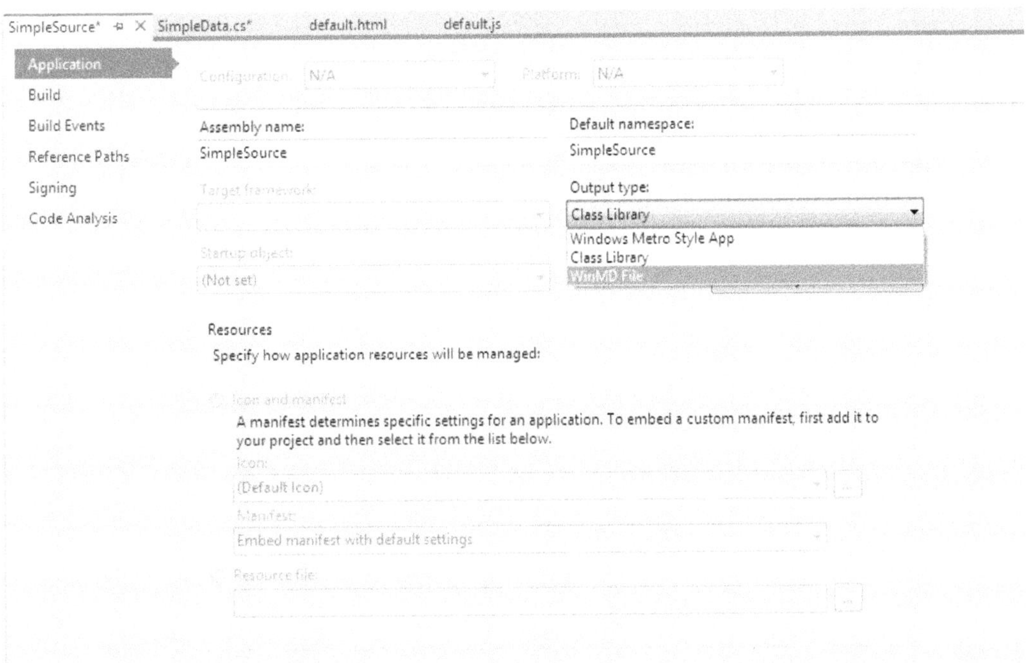

Figure 2-4. *Changing the project output type to WinMD*

5. Right-click the SimpleSource project and click Build to ensure everything is ready for use in the app.

Finish the JavaScript App

Now the WinRT component is ready for use. First, you must add a reference to the JavaScript project to the SimpleSource project.

1. Right-click Resources and click Add Reference, as shown in Figure 2-5.

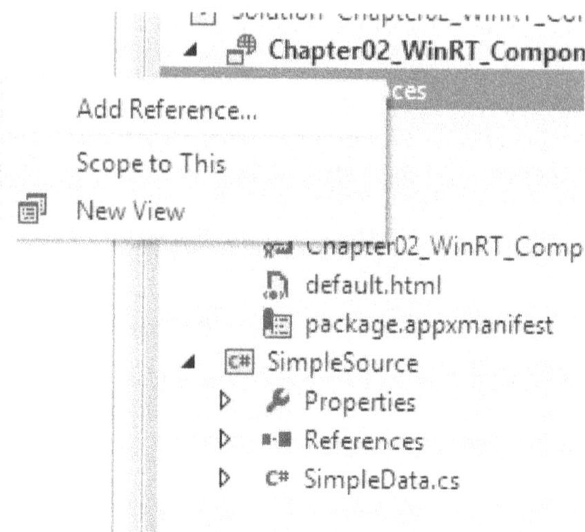

***Figure 2-5.** Adding a reference to the JavaScript project*

2. Select the SimpleSource reference from the Solution Projects list, as shown in Figure 2-6.

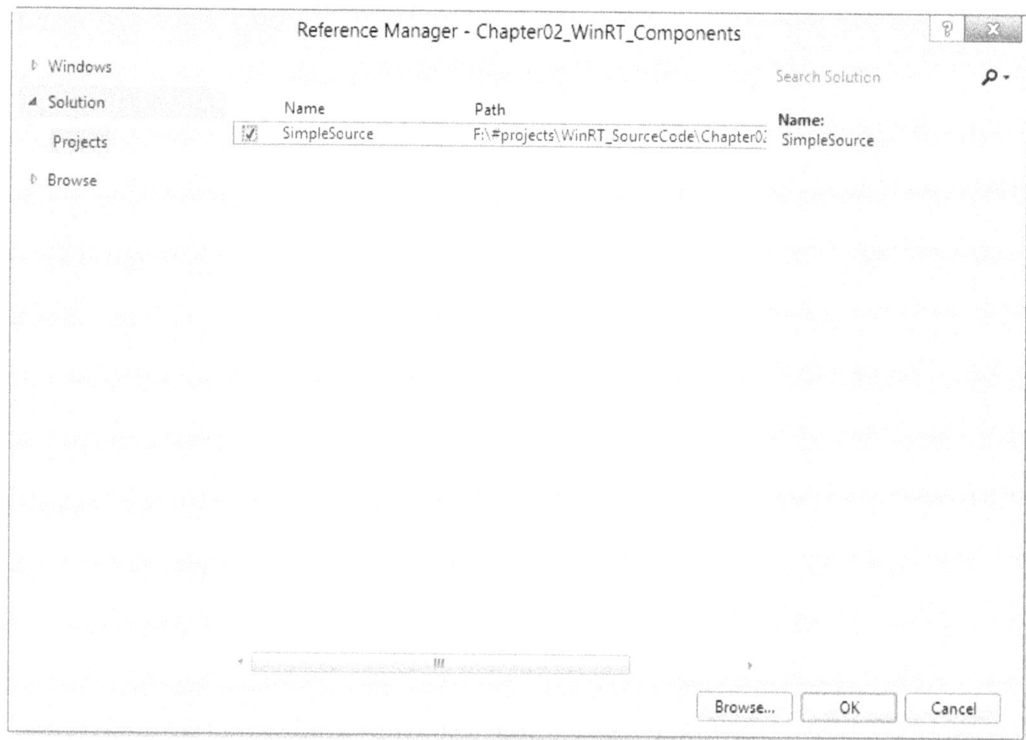

***Figure 2-6.** Adding a project reference to the JavaScript project*

All of the changes for this app will be on the main HTML page. You will add the JavaScript code directly to this file for simplicity. In a production-level app, you would typically organize your code into .js files and reference them in your HTML. Projects later in this book will take this approach, but this is the first simple app with a simple focus.

3. Open the **default.html** file.

4. Add `<div id="pageTitle"></div>` to the body of the page. This will be where the string returned from the WinRT component is displayed.

5. Add the following changes to the **default.css** file:

```
body {
        margin-left: 40px;
        margin-top: 40px;
}
...
#pageTitle {
        color: #000;
        font-size: 48px;
    }
```

6. Add the following script to the **default.html** file:

```
<script type="text/javascript">
    function onload() {
        var pageTitle = document.getElementById('pageTitle');
        pageTitle.textContent = new SimpleSource.SimpleData().appTitle;
    }
  </script>
```

This JavaScript function uses the WinRT component. Notice, the code simply looks like JavaScript. The `appTitle` property value is passed to the `textContext` property for display. None of the complexity that is required to make this work is of concern to you as the developer. It simply works.

7. Add `onload="onload();"` to the `<body>` tag of **default.html**.

The **default.html** page should now be complete. Check your code against Listing 2-2.

Listing 2-2. default.html

```
<!DOCTYPE html>
<html>
<head>
    <meta charset="utf-8">
    <title>Chapter02_WinRT_Components</title>

    <!-- WinJS references -->
    <link href="//Microsoft.WinJS.0.6/css/ui-light.css" rel="stylesheet">
    <script src="//Microsoft.WinJS.0.6/js/base.js"></script>
    <script src="//Microsoft.WinJS.0.6/js/ui.js"></script>

    <!-- Chapter02_WinRT_Components references -->
    <link href="/css/default.css" rel="stylesheet">
    <script src="/js/default.js"></script>

    <script type="text/javascript">
        function onload() {
```

```
            var pageTitle = document.getElementById('pageTitle');
            pageTitle.textContent = new SimpleSource.SimpleData().appTitle;
        }
    </script>
</head>
<body onload="onload();">
    <div id="pageTitle"></div>
</body>
</html>
```

8. Press F5 to run to app. It should load and your screen should look similar to Figure 2-7.

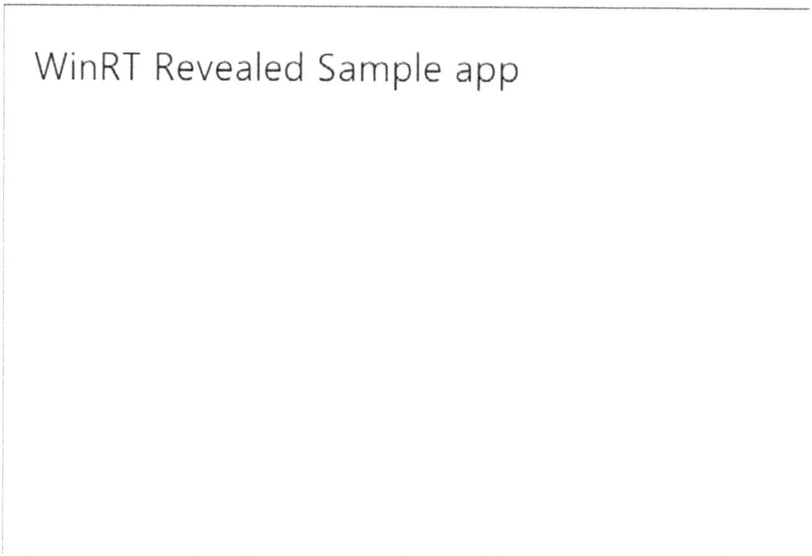

WinRT Revealed Sample app

Figure 2-7. *Sample app running*

■ **Note** You may notice that a new tile has been added to the Windows 8 Start screen. The app has been installed onto the machine, so a tile was created. Unfortunately, it is not a great looking one.

Enhance the App

So far, your JavaScript app simply demonstrates the mechanics of consuming a WinRT component. Now it is time to add some functionality and make your app a little more interesting.

You will add to the WinRT component a method that returns a list of dates based on a starting date and a number of days to add. The JavaScript app will add these dates to a drop-down list on the screen.

You will continue to work with the same solution as before. You will not need to create a new project.

Add a Method to the WinRT Component

You will start by enhancing the WinRT component. Start by adding the following method to the `SimpleData` class:

```
public IList<string> GetDates(string startDate, int days)
{
    List<string> dates = new List<string>();

    for (int count = 0; count <= days; count++)
    {
        dates.Add(DateTime.Parse(startDate).AddDays(
            Convert.ToDouble(count)).ToString("d")
        );
    }

    return dates;
}
```

Notice that the method returns a collection of type `IList<string>`. Remember, WinRT components must use WinRT types. The implementation of the method uses `List<string>`, but an `IList<string>` must be returned.

This method simply accepts a date (as a string) and an integer. It then returns a list of date strings by using the `startDate` and adding the number of days passed in.

Modify the JavaScript App

Now you can prepare the app to use the new method you added to your WinRT component. First, you need to make some changes to the UI to accept the necessary values from the user.

1. Add the following markup to **default.html** just below the existing `pageTitle` div:

```
<div id="inputValues" style="border">
        <div style="float: left;width: 200px;">
            Enter Start Date:
        </div>
        <div>
            <input id="txtStartDate" type="text" />
        </div>
        <div style="float: left;width: 200px;">
            Enter Number of Days:
        </div>
        <div>
            <input id="txtDayCount" type="text" />
        </div>
        <div style="float: left;width: 200px;"> </div>
        <div>
            <button onclick="getDates();">submit</button>
        </div>
  </div>
  <hr />
  <div id="main" style="margin-top: 20px;">
        <div style="float: left;width: 200px;">
          Date Options:
```

```
    </div>
    <select id="dateOptions" style="width: 200px;" />
</div>
```

This markup adds two text boxes for input and their labels. This code also includes the `select` control for displaying the output. A button allows the user to control the process, rather than simply loading some values when the page loads.

■ **Note** Visual Studio 11 Beta only provides a Source view for these pages. Since this is not a web app, but a Windows 8 Metro style app, there is no option to View in Browser, as you may be used to. However, you can view the page in Expression Blend. This is a good way to view the design, even if you choose not to use Blend to make the design changes.

Once the changes are made, the screen should look similar to Figure 2-8.

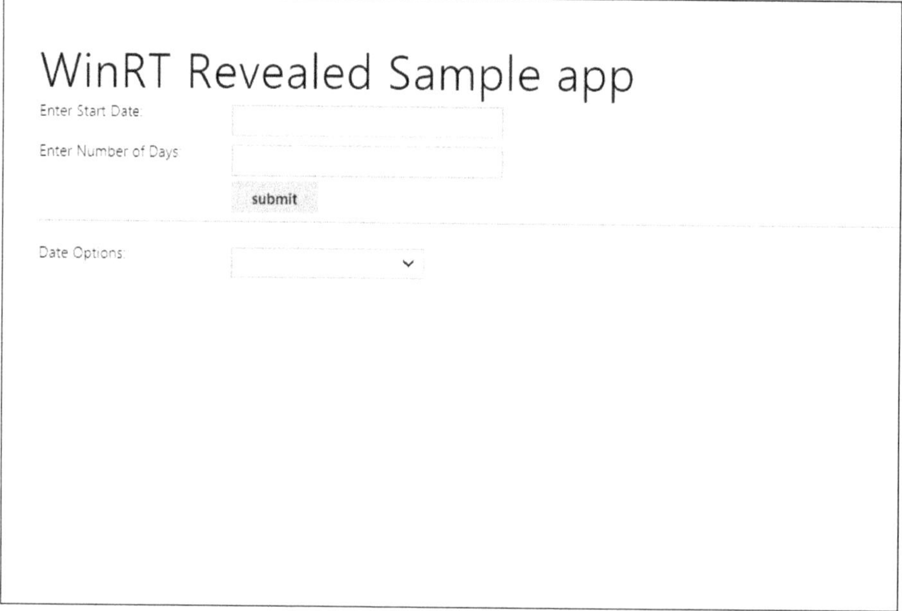

Figure 2-8. *Final default.html design*

2. Add the following JavaScript function to populate the `dateOptions` control. This function is called when the button on the screen is clicked.

```
function getDates() {
    var startDate = document.getElementById('txtStartDate').value;
    var dayCount = document.getElementById('txtDayCount').value;
```

```
        var dayList = new SimpleSource.SimpleData().getDates(
                    startDate, Number(dayCount)
                );

        var dateOptions = document.getElementById('dateOptions');

        //clear options
        dateOptions.options.length = 0;

        //load new options
        for (count = 0; count < dayList.length; count++) {
            dateOptions.options[dateOptions.options.length] =
                new Option(dayList[count]);
        }
    }
```

The function begins by getting the values from the input controls. Then the WinRT component is used, specifically calling the new method, `getDates()`. This returns an `IList<string>` from the component, which is essentially an array in JavaScript. The function then iterates through the array, adding each item to the `select` control.

To ensure that you didn't miss anything, review Listing 2-3, which contains the code from the **default.html** file after these changes.

Listing 2-3. default.html (Including the UI Elements)

```
<!DOCTYPE html>
<html>
<head>
    <meta charset="utf-8">
    <title>Chapter02_WinRT_Components</title>

    <!-- WinJS references -->
    <link href="//Microsoft.WinJS.0.6/css/ui-light.css" rel="stylesheet">
    <script src="//Microsoft.WinJS.0.6/js/base.js"></script>
    <script src="//Microsoft.WinJS.0.6/js/ui.js"></script>

    <!-- Chapter02_WinRT_Components references -->
    <link href="/css/default.css" rel="stylesheet">
    <script src="/js/default.js"></script>

    <script type="text/javascript">
      function onload() {
          var pageTitle = document.getElementById('pageTitle');
          pageTitle.textContent = new SimpleSource.SimpleData().appTitle;
      }

      function getDates() {
          var startDate = document.getElementById('txtStartDate').value;
          var dayCount = document.getElementById('txtDayCount').value;

          var dayList = new SimpleSource.SimpleData().getFollowingDates(
                      startDate, Number(dayCount)
                      );
```

```
        var dateOptions = document.getElementById('dateOptions');

        //clear options
        dateOptions.options.length = 0;

        //load new options
        for (count = 0; count < dayList.length; count++) {
             dateOptions.options[dateOptions.options.length] =
                          new Option(dayList[count]);
        }
      }
  </script>
</head>
<body onload="onload();">
  <div id="pageTitle"></div>

  <div id="inputValues" style="border">
    <div style="float: left;width: 200px;">
      Enter Start Date:
    </div>
    <div>
      <input id="txtStartDate" type="text" />
    </div>
    <div style="float: left;width: 200px;">
      Enter Number of Days:
    </div>
    <div>
       <input id="txtDayCount" type="text" />
    </div>
    <div style="float: left;width: 200px;"> </div>
    <div>
      <button onclick="getDates();">submit</button>
    </div>
  </div>
  <hr />
  <div id="main" style="margin-top: 20px;">
    <div style="float: left;width: 200px;">
      Date Options:
    </div>
    <select id="dateOptions" style="width: 200px;" />
  </div>
</body>
</html>
```

3. Press F5 to run the app. Enter some values into the input boxes and click the **submit** button. Your screen should appear similar to Figure 2-9.

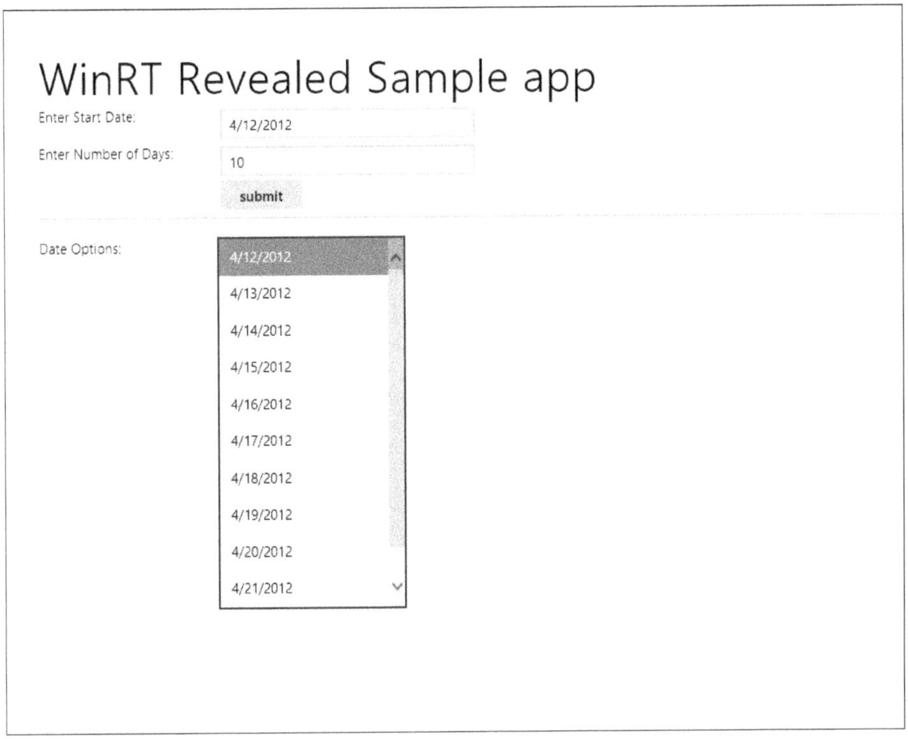

Figure 2-9. Sample app running, populated with dates from input

Access the Windows Namespace

You have seen that it is very simple to build a WinRT component and use it in an app. However, Microsoft designed WinRT to be used directly in your apps. Now you will add a simple control to your app to demonstrate this.

You will add a drop-down list that will show all of the devices on your machine. To get this list, you will access the `Windows.Devices` namespace.

1. Modify the HTML markup to include the UI controls for displaying the list of devices. Add the following HTML to the **default.html** file, within the <body> tag, just after the existing code:

```
<hr />
 <div id="deviceSection" style="margin-top: 20px;">
   <div style="float: left;width: 200px;">
     <button onclick="loadDevices();">load</button>
   </div>
   <select id="deviceOptions"></select>
 </div>
```

This markup adds a button and a drop-down list to the screen. The button is used to simply control when the drop-down list is loaded. Now your screen should appear similar to Figure 2-10.

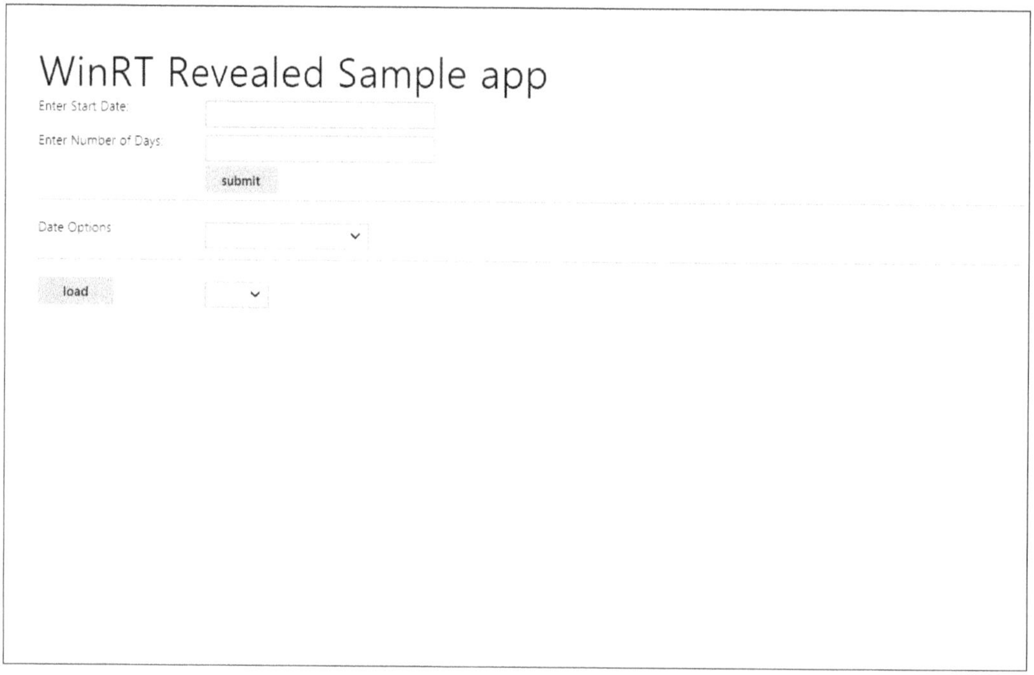

Figure 2-10. *Sample app design with added device list controls*

2. Add the following JavaScript function for loading the devices. This function is called when the button is clicked.

```
function loadDevices() {
      //add list of devices
      var deviceList = Windows.Devices.Enumeration.DeviceInformation;
      deviceList.findAllAsync(
  Windows.Devices.Enumeration.DeviceClass.all).then(
          onSuccess,
          onError
        );
}
```

This function uses the `Windows.Devices` namespace to find all of the devices on your machine. The `findAllAsync()` method returns the desired list. This method requires callback methods for success and failure.

3. Add the following functions to handle these events:

```
function onSuccess(deviceCollection) {
     var numDevices = deviceCollection.length;
     var options = document.getElementById('deviceOptions');

     for (var count = 0; count < numDevices; count++) {
         var device = deviceCollection[count];
         options.options[options.options.length] =
             new Option(device.name);
      }
}
```

```
        function onError(e) {
            //do nothing
        }
```

The `onSuccess()` method loads the drop-down list with the items returned. A `DeviceInformationCollection` object is returned by the `findAllAsync()` method. This function simply iterates through the collection and adds each item to the drop-down list.

The `onError()` method does nothing, as this app is simply for demonstration. Production-focused code would obviously take care of things like error handling.

4. Press F5 to run the app.

When you click the **load** button, you should see a long list of devices added to the drop-down list control. This list is not very useful, but again, this is simply for demonstration. Your screen should look similar to Figure 2-11.

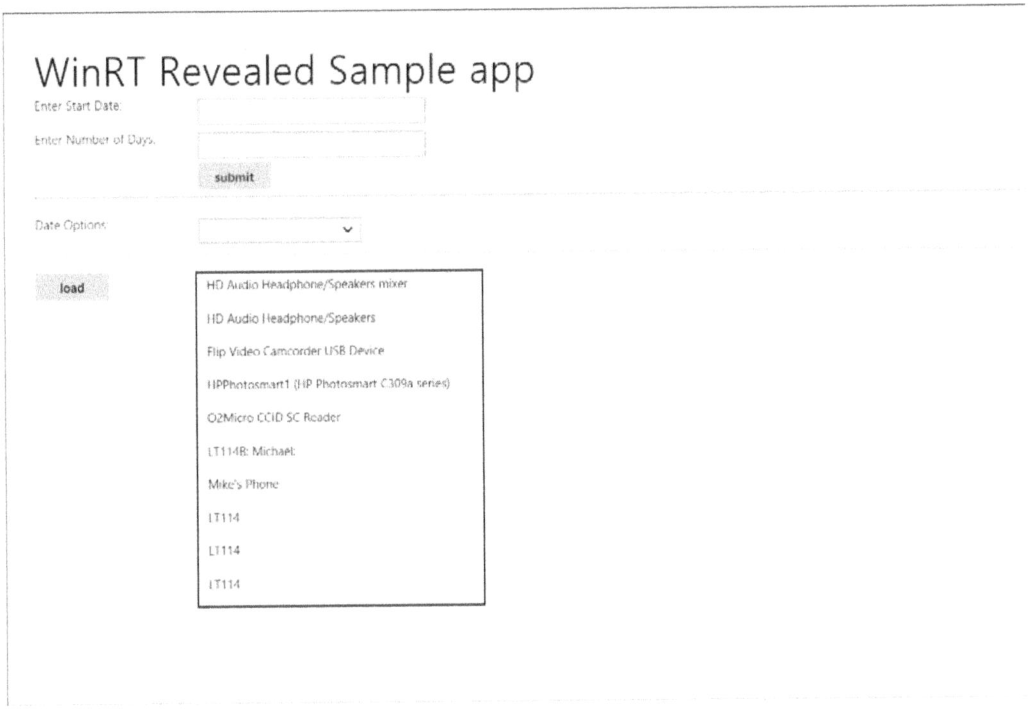

Figure 2-11. *Sample app running with devices loaded*

Listing 2-4 contains the final version of **default.html**.

Listing 2-4. The Final Version of default.html

```
<!DOCTYPE html>
<html>
<head>
    <meta charset="utf-8">
    <title>Chapter02_WinRT_Components</title>
```

```
<!-- WinJS references -->
<link href="//Microsoft.WinJS.0.6/css/ui-light.css" rel="stylesheet">
<script src="//Microsoft.WinJS.0.6/js/base.js"></script>
<script src="//Microsoft.WinJS.0.6/js/ui.js"></script>

<!-- Chapter02_WinRT_Components references -->
<link href="/css/default.css" rel="stylesheet">
<script src="/js/default.js"></script>

<script type="text/javascript">
    function onload() {
        var pageTitle = document.getElementById('pageTitle');
    pageTitle.textContent = new SimpleSource.SimpleData().appTitle;
  }

  function getDates() {
    var startDate = document.getElementById('txtStartDate').value;
    var dayCount = document.getElementById('txtDayCount').value;

    var dayList = new SimpleSource.SimpleData().getDates(startDate, Number(dayCount));

    var dateOptions = document.getElementById('dateOptions');

    //clear options
    dateOptions.options.length = 0;

    //load new options
    for (count = 0; count < dayList.length; count++) {
        dateOptions.options[dateOptions.options.length] =
               new Option(dayList[count]);
    }
  }

  function loadDevices() {
      //add list of devices
      var deviceList = Windows.Devices.Enumeration.DeviceInformation;
      deviceList.findAllAsync(
      Windows.Devices.Enumeration.DeviceClass.all).then(
              onSuccess,
              onError
      );
  }

  function onSuccess(deviceCollection) {
      var numDevices = deviceCollection.length;
      var options = document.getElementById('deviceOptions');

      for (var count = 0; count < numDevices; count++) {
          var device = deviceCollection[count];

          options.options[options.options.length] =
             new Option(device.name);
               }
          }

          function onError(e) {
            //do nothing
          }
</script>
```

```
</head>
<body onload="onload();">
  <div>
      <div id="pageTitle"></div>

      <div id="inputValues" style="border">
          <div style="float: left;width: 200px;">
              Enter Start Date:
          </div>
          <div>
              <input id="txtStartDate" type="text" />
          </div>
          <div style="float: left;width: 200px;">
              Enter Number of Days:
          </div>
          <div>
               <input id="txtDayCount" type="text" />
          </div>
          <div style="float: left;width: 200px;"> </div>
          <div>
              <button onclick="getDates();">submit</button>
          </div>
      </div>
      <hr />
      <div id="output" style="margin-top: 20px;">
        <div style="float: left;width: 200px;">
            Date Options:
        </div>
        <select id="dateOptions" style="width: 200px;"></select>
      </div>
      <hr />
      <div id="deviceSection" style="margin-top: 20px;">
          <div style="float: left;width: 200px;">
             <button onclick="loadDevices();">load</button>
          </div>
          <select id="deviceOptions"></select>
      </div>
    </div>
</body>
</html>
```

Summary

You have seen how WinRT components can be built using the .NET language of Visual C#. You built your own component and used it in a Windows 8 Metro style app, written in HTML and JavaScript. This process is very simple and everything remains familiar when working with any of the languages.

You have also peeked into the Windows namespace to use built-in WinRT functionality in your app. The rest of the book will focus deeper on WinRT functionality and how to use it in your apps.

CHAPTER 3

Building a .NET App with WinRT

Chapter 2 focused on building components and accessing them across languages. For many scenarios, this will come in handy. However, the vast majority of development situations will use the controls and components included in Windows 8.

This chapter focuses on a few of the simpler controls and consumes them into a .NET app written in Visual C#. Developers with knowledge of WPF or Silverlight will find this chapter quite familiar.

In this chapter you will

- Build a Visual C# Metro style app
- Consume Windows 8 WinRT controls and components
- Use data binding to populate WinRT controls
- Use templating to control the display of data

Note Visual C# was chosen for this chapter in order to utilize XAML controls and demonstrate .NET development against WinRT. At the very least, it extends the range of exposure from the previous chapter, which focused on HTML and JavaScript

---

A Simple Design

The app in this chapter is for demonstration purposes only, so the design is simple. The app will show a couple of different ways to access the photos on your machine. It will demonstrate data binding and control manipulation. The basic features and approaches shown in this chapter will work for nearly all WinRT controls.

There are many resources, online and in print, that focus on building Metro style apps. This chapter is not about the design aspects and other points of interest when building an app for the Windows Marketplace. The focus of this chapter is WinRT and showing you how to use it.

Note You can find a list of resources for building Windows 8 Metro style apps in the appendix of this book.

Create the Solution

In this section, you will start with the Blank Application template and build an app that demonstrates some fundamental concepts of working with WinRT controls. You will add data binding and control manipulation.

1. Start Visual Studio 11 Beta on your Windows 8 development machine.
2. Create a new project and select the Blank Application template in the Visual C# Windows Metro style section.
3. Enter the name of your solution and the location for your code files. When your screen is similar to Figure 3-1, click OK.

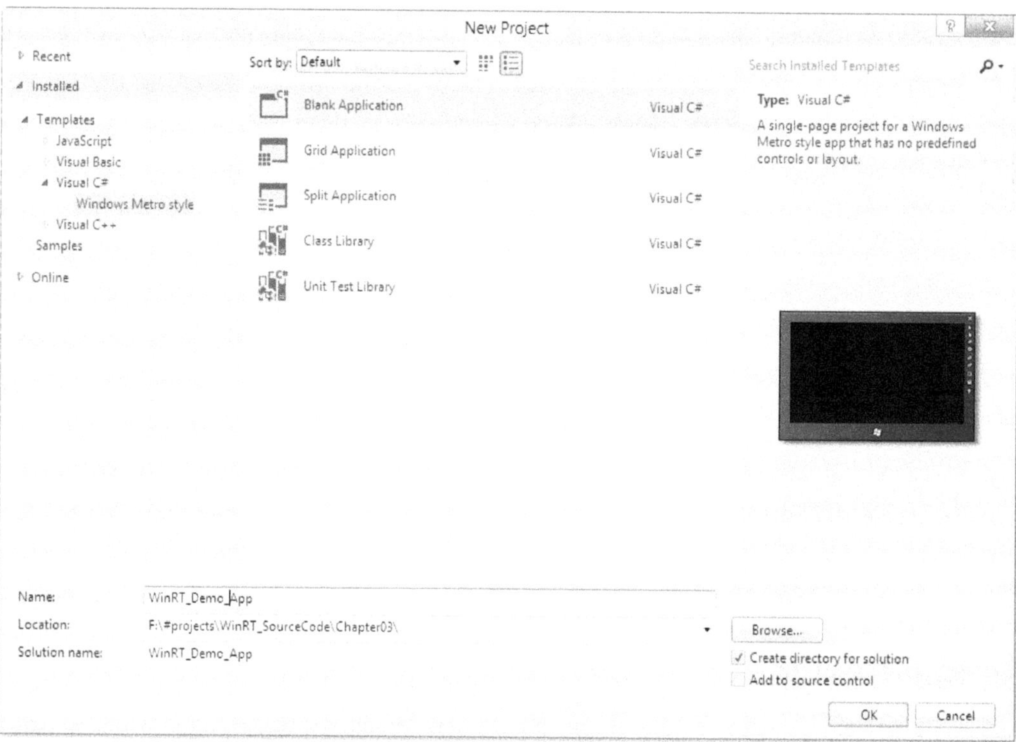

***Figure 3-1.** Creating a new Visual C# Metro style project*

Visual Studio creates the solution and necessary project files for your app. You will begin by building the UI, so look for the **BlankPage.xaml** file.

Build the UI

Every good app starts with the user experience.

1. Open the **BlankPage.xaml** file. The page consists of an empty `Grid` control. Replace the `Grid` control with the following code:

```
<Grid Background="Silver">
    <Grid.RowDefinitions>
      <RowDefinition />
      <RowDefinition />
    </Grid.RowDefinitions>
    <Grid.ColumnDefinitions>
      <ColumnDefinition />
      <ColumnDefinition />
    </Grid.ColumnDefinitions>
  </Grid>
```

This XAML simply sets up the structure of the page. It breaks up the screen into four even areas. Now you will add the controls for each area.

2. Add the following code just above the closing Grid tag to build the controls for the top left section of the screen:

```
<StackPanel Grid.Column="0" Grid.Row="0" VerticalAlignment="Center">
   <TextBlock FontSize="40" HorizontalAlignment="Center"
      VerticalAlignment="Top">
         Test App
   </TextBlock>
     <ComboBox x:Name="cboOptions" Width="400" Margin="20"
     SelectionChanged="cboOptions_SelectionChanged_1">
   </ComboBox>
     <Button x:Name="btnPickImage" Width="200" Content="Change Image"
      HorizontalAlignment="Center" Click="btnPickImage_Click_1" />
         </StackPanel>
```

The design view in Visual Studio should appear similar to Figure 3-2.

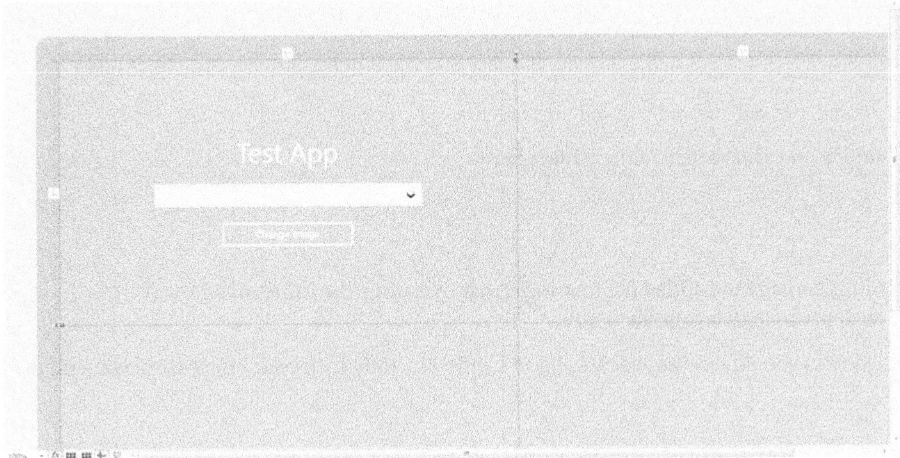

Figure 3-2. *Design view of the first set of controls*

This section arranges the controls on the top left using a StackPanel control. The values of Grid.Column and Grid.Row specify where the controls display in the Grid control. The StackPanel control is in column "0" and row "0."

Within the StackPanel control, there is a TextBlock control to display the title for the app, a ComboBox control to display a few options for interaction by the user, and a Button control for the user to click.

3. Add an Image control to the top right section. Add the following code just below the StackPanel control:

```
<Image x:Name="imgPhoto" Grid.Column="1" Grid.Row="0"
   Source="images/image1.jpg" Height="300" Width="300">
</Image>
```

The Image control references a file in the Source attribute. This file needs to be added to the project to display on the screen.

4. Right click on the solution and click Add ➤ New Folder. Name the new folder "images".

5. Add an image file from your machine by clicking the images folder and selecting Add ➤ Existing Item, as shown in Figure 3-3.

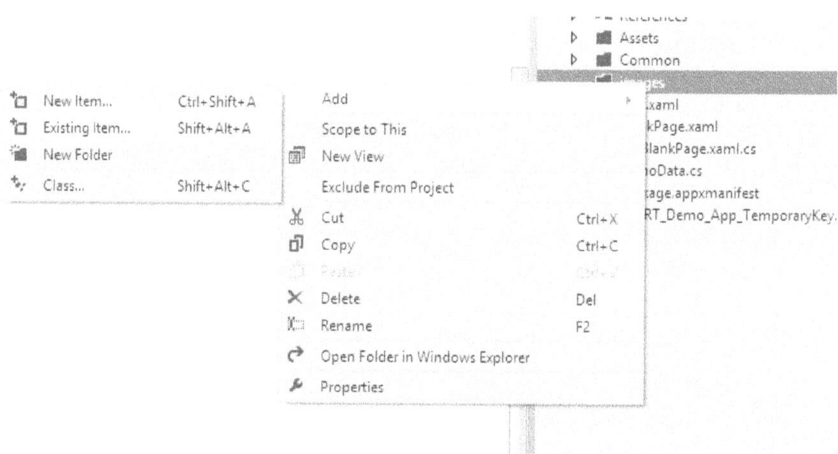

Figure 3-3. *Adding an existing item to the images folder*

6. Either rename the added file to **image1.jpg** or change the value of the Source attribute to match your file name.

The design view should now appear similar to Figure 3-4, only with your image displaying on the top right.

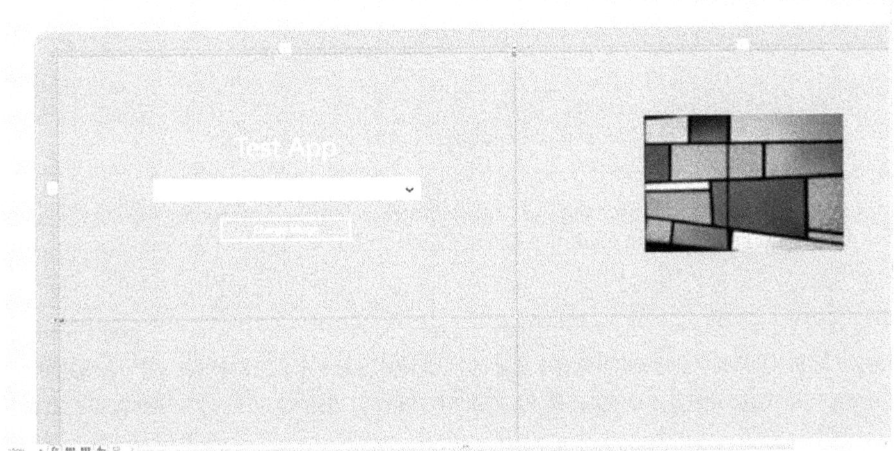

Figure 3-4. *Design view after controls defined for both top sections*

Make the App Work

The UI for the top half of the app is complete. Now you will focus on making this section actually work before you turn to concentrating on the rest of the app. You will start with the `Combo Box` control of options.

You will use data binding to populate the `Combo Box` control. For data binding, you need a data source.

1. Right-click the solution and click Add Class. Name the class **DemoData.cs**. Add the code from Listing 3-1 to this new file.

Listing 3-1. DemoData.cs

```
public static class DemoData
{
    public static List<string> GetSizeOptions()
    {
        List<string> options = new List<string>();

        options.Add("Small");
        options.Add("Medium");
        options.Add("Large");
        return options;
    }
}
```

This class has one simple method, `GetSizeOptions()`. This method returns a `List<>` of string objects. This will be used as the options for the `Combo Box` control.

2. Open **BlankPage.xaml.cs**. Add the following `using` statements to the beginning of the class file:

```
using Windows.Storage.Pickers;
using Windows.UI.Xaml.Media.Imaging;
using Windows.Storage;
```

3. Add the following method to the class:

```
void BlankPage_Loaded(object sender, RoutedEventArgs e)
{
      //bind data to control
      cboOptions.ItemsSource = DemoData.GetSizeOptions();
}
```

This method simply binds `cboOptions` to the `List<>` of strings that is returned by the `SetSizeOptions()` method. Since the method returns a collection of strings, the combo box will use the value as the display and the value of each item.

■ **Note** You can bind a collection of other types to a control like `Combo Box`. However, you would need to set the `DisplayMember` and `ValueMember` properties to configure how to display and work with items bound to the control.

The method needs to be called. In fact, the method `BlankPage_Loaded()` is actually an event handler, written to be called once the page is loaded.

4. Add the following line of code to the `BlankPage()` constructor, just after the `this.InitializeComponent()` line:

```
this.Loaded += BlankPage_Loaded;
```

5. Add the following code to handle the event when the selection in the `Combo Box` control is changed:

```
private void cboOptions_SelectionChanged_1(object sender,
   SelectionChangedEventArgs e)
     {
       switch (e.AddedItems[0].ToString())
       {
           case "Small":
               imgPhoto.Height = 100;
               imgPhoto.Width = 100;
               break;
           case "Medium":
               imgPhoto.Height = 300;
               imgPhoto.Width = 300;
               break;
           case "Large":
               imgPhoto.Height = 600;
               imgPhoto.Width = 600;
               break;
       }
    }
```

This code changes the size of the `Image` control based on the selection made by the user.

6. Add the following code to handle the button click event for `btnPickImage`:

```
async private void btnPickImage_Click_1(object sender, RoutedEventArgs e)
{
    var filePicker = new FileOpenPicker();
    filePicker.FileTypeFilter.Add(".jpg");
    filePicker.ViewMode = PickerViewMode.Thumbnail;
    filePicker.SuggestedStartLocation = PickerLocationId.PicturesLibrary;
    filePicker.SettingsIdentifier = "imagePicker";
    filePicker.CommitButtonText = "Choose an image to load";

    var file = await filePicker.PickSingleFileAsync();

    BitmapImage bitmap = new BitmapImage();
    bitmap.SetSource(
       await file.OpenAsync(Windows.Storage.FileAccessMode.Read)
  );
    imgPhoto.Source = bitmap;
}
```

This is the most complex section of code so far. This method uses the WinRT `FilePicker` control. When the button is clicked, a new instance of the `FilePicker` is instantiated. Settings are configured.

■ **Note** The `FileTypeFilter` property needs at least one value added, even if that value is `""`.

The `CommitButtonText` property allows you to override the `FilePicker` button text.

Chapter 1 explained that WinRT was designed to run asynchronously most of the time. The `FilePicker` runs this way. The `await` keyword is used to allow the code to open the `FilePicker` and wait for the response without stopping the UI thread from working, as in the following line from this method:

```
var file = await filePicker.PickSingleFileAsync();
```

Adding an `await` statement into a method does require that method to run asynchronously as well. You can see that the `async` keyword has been added to the method definition to satisfy this requirement.

Once the file is chosen by the user, it is then read into a `BitmapImage` object for display on the screen.

These are the last of the code changes for the top sections of this app. You can refer to Listing 3-3 toward the end of this chapter if you have questions regarding code placement in the files.

Run the First Test

Now you are ready to run the app.

1. Press F5 to run the solution. Your screen should appear similar to Figure 3-5.

Figure 3-5. *WinRT_Demo_App running in first test*

2. The Combo Box control should be populated with the options shown in Figure 3-6.

Figure 3-6. *WinRT_Demo_App Combo Box options*

3. Selecting an option in the Combo Box control should change the size of the image, as shown in Figure 3-7.

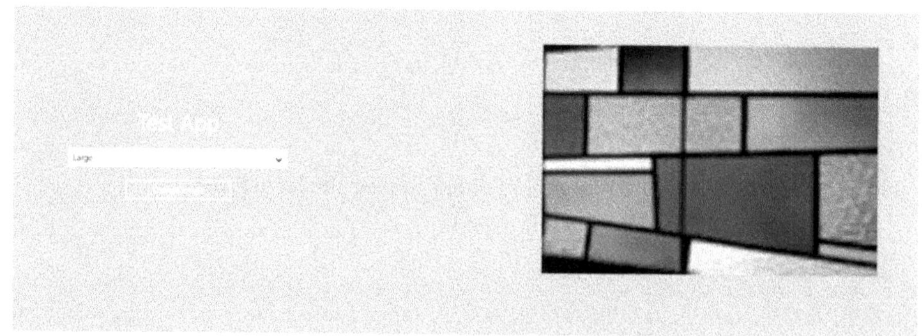

Figure 3-7. *WinRT_Demo_App with image resized*

4. Clicking the **Change Image** button should bring up the File Picker. Your screen should look similar to Figure 3-8.

Figure 3-8. *WinRT File Picker (images blurred intentionally)*

5. Choose a file and click the **Choose and image to load** button, as shown in Figure 3-9.

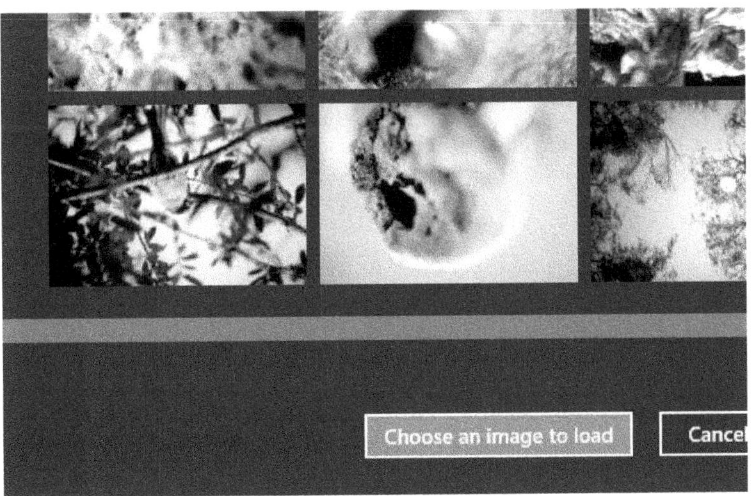

Figure 3-9. *File Picker button*

The image you chose should appear on the right side of the screen. You can continue to resize this image with the Combo Box control, or you can choose other files to load in its place.

■ **Note** This app uses the `FilePicker` to gain access to files on the machine. This interaction involves the user, so permission is granted. If the app were to load a file directly, without interaction from the user, the app would need to be configured to do so. This is done by managing the Capabilities list in the **`Package.appxmanifest`** file. Figure 3-10 shows this file and the options available.

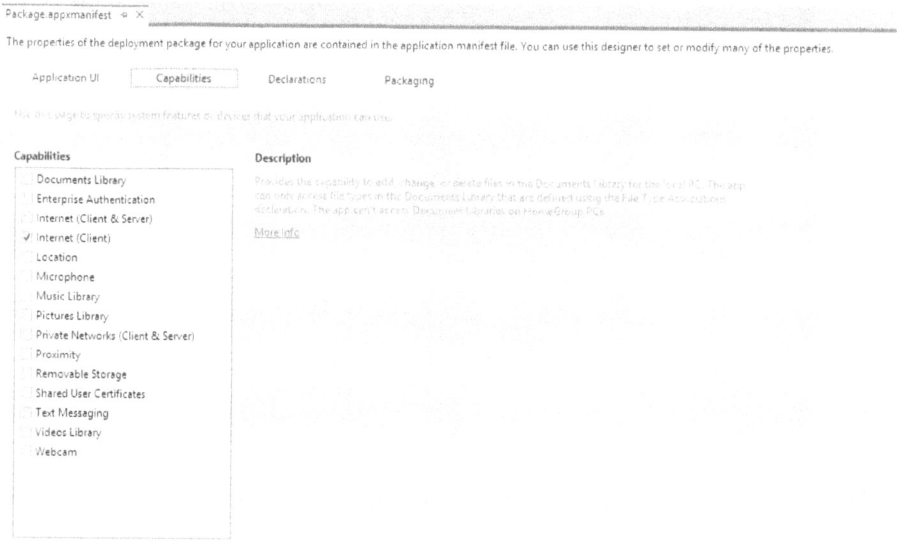

Figure 3-10. *Managing the capabilities of an app*

Complete the UI

Now you will add the UI markup for the bottom sections of the screen.

1. Open **BlankPage.xaml** and add the following code just below the `StackPanel` control added earlier:

```
<Button Grid.Column="0" Grid.Row="1" x:Name="btnPickFolder" Width="200"
   Content="Load images from folder" HorizontalAlignment="Center"
   Click="btnPickFolder_Click_1" />
<GridView x:Name="gvPhotos" Grid.Column="1" Grid.Row="1"
   HorizontalAlignment="Stretch" Margin="0" VerticalAlignment="Stretch"
   ItemTemplate="{StaticResource Standard250x250ItemTemplate}">
</GridView>
```

This XAML markup adds a `Button` control to the bottom left section and a `GridView` control to the bottom right section. The button is configured to look just like the button in the top section. The `GridView` control is configured to fill the bottom right section. It also is set up to use the `Standard250x250ItemTemplate` template.

■ **Note** The `Standard250x250ItemTemplate` template is provided by the default Metro style files. It can be found in the solution under the Common folder, in the **`StandardStyles.xaml`** file.

The UI is now complete. The design view in Visual Studio should appear similar to Figure 3-11. While the `GridView` control is present, there is no visible element until the data is added. Therefore, it does not appear in the design view.

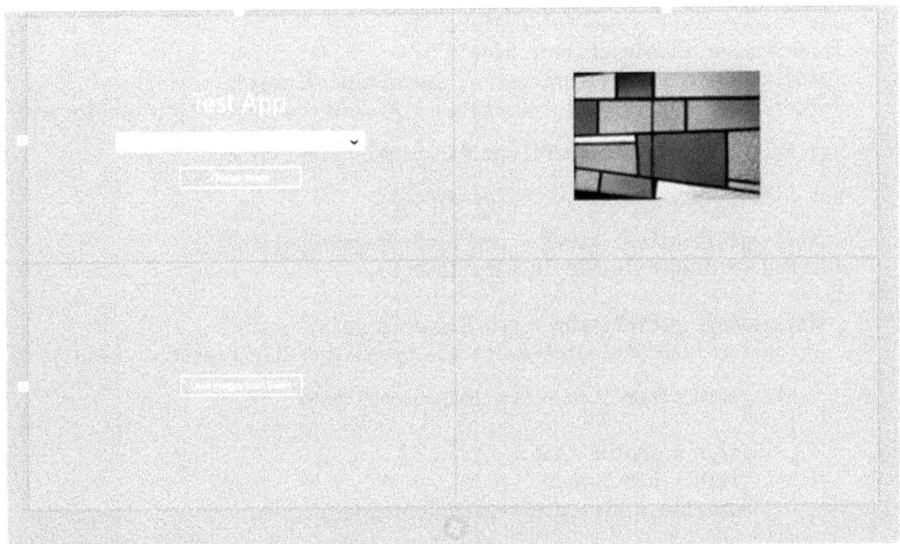

Figure 3-11. *Complete UI design*

Complete the App

The data template for the items in the `GridView` control requires an object with particular properties.

1. Add a new class file to the solution called **ImageGroupItem.cs**. The code for this class file is shown in Listing 3-2.

Listing 3-2. ImageGroupItem.cs

```
using System;
using System.Collections.Generic;
using System.Linq;
using System.Text;
using System.Threading.Tasks;

using Windows.UI.Xaml.Media.Imaging;

namespace WinRT_Demo_App
{
  class ImageGroupItem
```

```
    {
        public BitmapImage Image { get; set; }
        public string Title { get; set; }
        public string Subtitle { get; set; }
    }
}
```

2. Add the following code to handle the button click event for btnPickFolder:

```
async private void btnPickFolder_Click_1(object sender, RoutedEventArgs e)
{

    var folderPicker = new FolderPicker();
    folderPicker.FileTypeFilter.Add("*");
    folderPicker.SettingsIdentifier = "imageFolderPicker";
    folderPicker.SuggestedStartLocation = PickerLocationId.PicturesLibrary;

    var folder = await folderPicker.PickSingleFolderAsync();

    var files = await folder.GetFilesAsync();

    List<ImageGroupItem> items = new List<ImageGroupItem>();
    foreach (StorageFile file in files.Take(6))
    {
      BitmapImage photoBitmap = new BitmapImage();
         photoBitmap.SetSource(await file.OpenAsync(FileAccessMode.Read));

         ImageGroupItem item = new ImageGroupItem()
        {
            Image = photoBitmap,
            Title = file.Name,
            Subtitle = file.DateCreated.ToString()
        };

        items.Add(item);
    }

  gvPhotos.ItemsSource = items;
}
```

This method uses the FolderPicker WinRT control. It works very similarly to the FilePicker used earlier. Once a folder is chosen, the code loops through the files and creates a list of ImageGroupItem objects and binds that list to the GridView control.

The asynchronous methods GetSingleFolderAsync() and GetFilesAsync() are used in this section. Prior to C# 4.5, a separate method would need to be implemented to handle the response from the asynchronous call. In C# 4.5, the await keyword is available. Asynchronous development has become straightforward and simple.

In this example, the files and folders will be retrieved without causing the UI layer to stop responding to the user. The async keyword is required on the method signature because the await keyword is used.

■ **Note** The Take(6) method on the files collection is used to control the number of images bound to the GridView control. Depending on the size of the images in the folder chosen, performance can become a problem with a large number of images.

Run Final Tests

The app is ready for complete functionality tests.

1. Press F5 to run the app. You should see something similar to Figure 3-12.

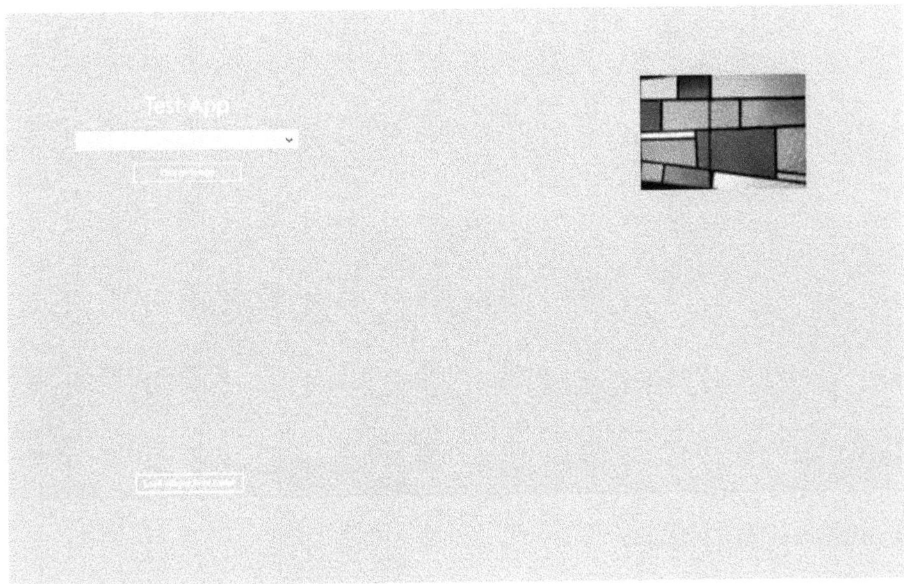

Figure 3-12. *WinRT_Demo_App running for final tests*

2. Click the **Load images from folder** button on the bottom of the screen to bring up the `FolderPicker`, as shown in Figure 3-13.

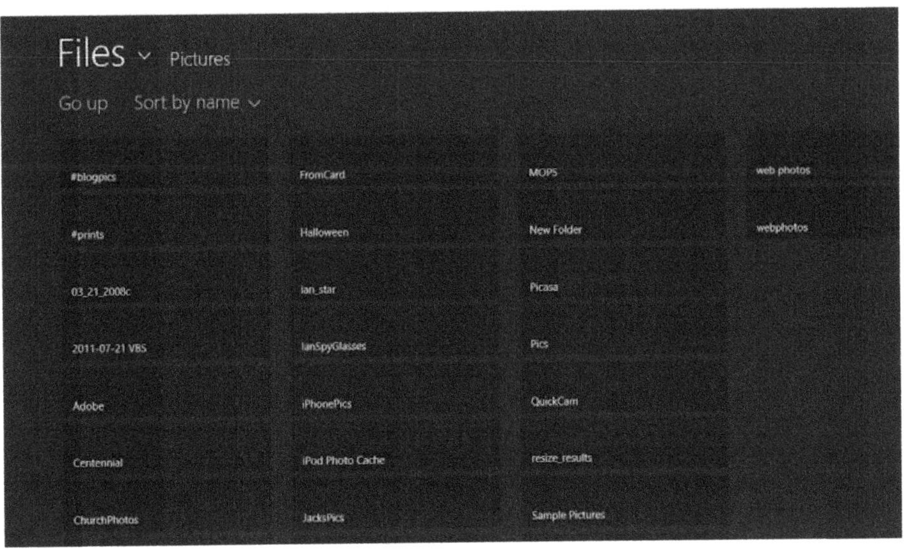

Figure 3-13. *WinRT FolderPicker*

3. Choose a folder and click the **Choose this folder** button at the bottom, shown in Figure 3-14.

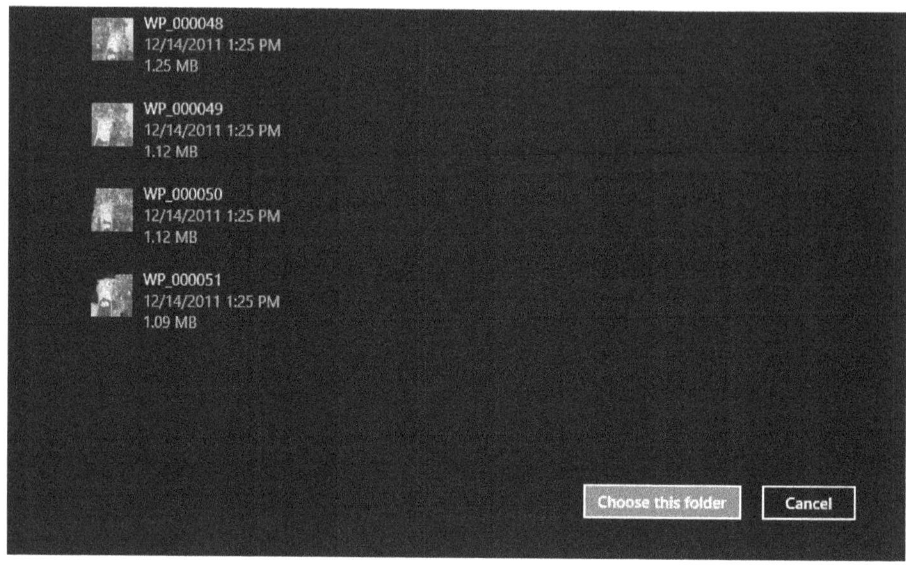

Figure 3-14. *FolderPicker commit button*

Six images from the chosen folder should load into the `GridView` control with their information, as shown in Figure 3-15.

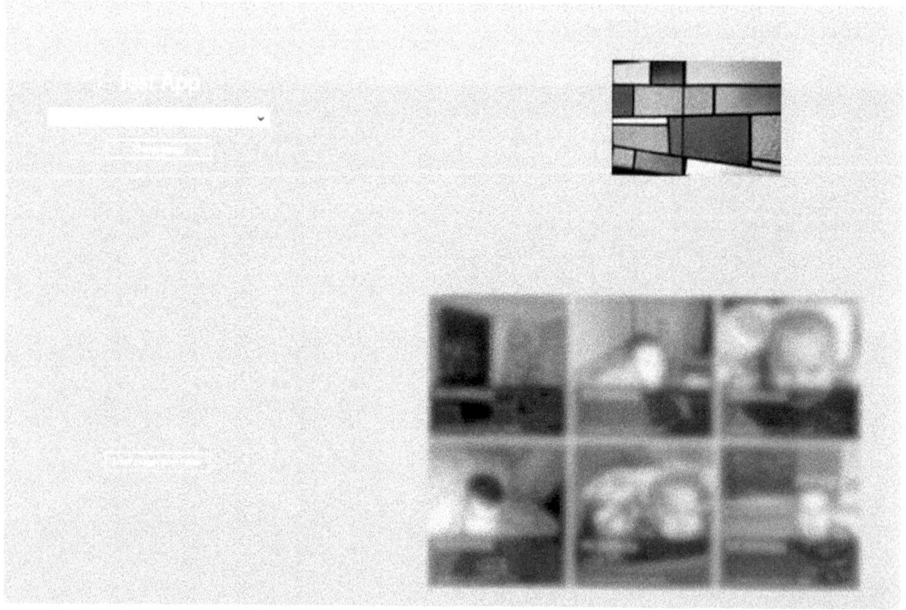

Figure 3-15. *Images loaded into GridView (blurring intentional)*

The full code for **BlankPage.xaml** is included in Listing 3-3. If you are not familiar with XAML, it is helpful to see how the markup works. The Grid control includes column and row definitions to break up the screen into areas. StackPanel controls help to organize controls within an area. It is in the XAML that the UI layer is described.

Listing 3-3. BlankPage.xaml

```
<Page
    x:Class="WinRT_Demo_App.BlankPage"

xmlns="http://schemas.microsoft.com/winfx/2006/xaml/presentation"

    xmlns:x="http://schemas.microsoft.com/winfx/2006/xaml"
    xmlns:local="using:WinRT_Demo_App"
    xmlns:d="http://schemas.microsoft.com/expression/blend/2008"
    xmlns:mc="http://schemas.openxmlformats.org/markup-compatibility/2006"
    mc:Ignorable="d">
    <Grid Background="Silver">
      <Grid.RowDefinitions>
          <RowDefinition />
          <RowDefinition />
      </Grid.RowDefinitions>
      <Grid.ColumnDefinitions>
          <ColumnDefinition />
          <ColumnDefinition />
      </Grid.ColumnDefinitions>
      <StackPanel Grid.Column="0" Grid.Row="0" VerticalAlignment="Center">
        <TextBlock FontSize="40" HorizontalAlignment="Center"
         VerticalAlignment="Top">Test App</TextBlock>
        <ComboBox x:Name="cboOptions" Width="400" Margin="20"
         SelectionChanged="cboOptions_SelectionChanged_1"></ComboBox>
        <Button x:Name="btnPickImage" Width="200" Content="Change image"
         HorizontalAlignment="Center" Click="btnPickImage_Click_1" />
      </StackPanel>
      <Image x:Name="imgPhoto" Grid.Column="1" Grid.Row="0"
       Source="images/image1.jpg" Height="300" Width="300"></Image>
      <Button Grid.Column="0" Grid.Row="1" x:Name="btnPickFolder"
       Width="200" Content="Load images from folder"
       HorizontalAlignment="Center" Click="btnPickFolder_Click_1" />
      <GridView x:Name="gvPhotos" Grid.Column="1" Grid.Row="1"
       HorizontalAlignment="Stretch" Margin="0"
       VerticalAlignment="Stretch"
       ItemTemplate="{StaticResource Standard250x250ItemTemplate}">
              </GridView>
    </Grid>
</Page>
```

The full code for **BlankPage.xaml.cs** is included in Listing 3-4. If you run into any issues building the project, check here to ensure that your code is correct and is in the correct place. This code is straightforward. It is essentially a collection of event handlers. There are no real tricks here, but that is by design. Developing with WinRT is straightforward.

Listing 3-4. BlankPage.xaml.cs

```
using System;
using System.Collections.Generic;
using System.IO;
using System.Linq;
using Windows.Foundation;
using Windows.Foundation.Collections;
using Windows.UI.Xaml;
using Windows.UI.Xaml.Controls;
using Windows.UI.Xaml.Controls.Primitives;
using Windows.UI.Xaml.Data;
using Windows.UI.Xaml.Input;
using Windows.UI.Xaml.Media;
using Windows.UI.Xaml.Navigation;

using Windows.Storage.Pickers;
using Windows.UI.Xaml.Media.Imaging;
using Windows.Storage;

// The Blank Page item template is documented at http://go.microsoft.com/fwlink/?LinkId=234238

namespace WinRT_Demo_App
{
    /// <summary>
    /// An empty page that can be used on its own or navigated to within a Frame.
    /// </summary>
    public sealed partial class BlankPage : Page
    {

       public BlankPage()
    {
        this.InitializeComponent();
        this.Loaded += BlankPage_Loaded;
    }

    void BlankPage_Loaded(object sender, RoutedEventArgs e)
    {
        //bind data to control
        cboOptions.ItemsSource = DemoData.GetSizeOptions();
    }

    /// <summary>
    /// Invoked when this page is about to be displayed in a Frame.
    /// </summary>
    /// <param name="e">Event data that describes how this page was reached. The Parameter
    /// property is typically used to configure the page.</param>
    protected override void OnNavigatedTo(NavigationEventArgs e)
    {
    }

    private void cboOptions_SelectionChanged_1(object sender, SelectionChangedEventArgs e)
    {
        switch (e.AddedItems[0].ToString())
```

```
    {
        case "Small":
            imgPhoto.Height = 100;
            imgPhoto.Width = 100;
            break;
        case "Medium":
            imgPhoto.Height = 300;
            imgPhoto.Width = 300;
            break;
        case "Large":
            imgPhoto.Height = 600;
            imgPhoto.Width = 600;
            break;
   }
}
async private void btnPickImage_Click_1(object sender, RoutedEventArgs e)
{
    var filePicker = new FileOpenPicker();
    filePicker.FileTypeFilter.Add(".jpg");
    filePicker.ViewMode = PickerViewMode.Thumbnail;
    filePicker.SuggestedStartLocation = PickerLocationId.PicturesLibrary;
    filePicker.SettingsIdentifier = "imagePicker";
    filePicker.CommitButtonText = "Choose an image to load";

    var file = await filePicker.PickSingleFileAsync();

    BitmapImage bitmap = new BitmapImage();
    bitmap.SetSource(await file.OpenAsync(Windows.Storage.FileAccessMode.Read));
    imgPhoto.Source = bitmap;
}
async private void btnPickFolder_Click_1(object sender, RoutedEventArgs e)
{
    var folderPicker = new FolderPicker();
    folderPicker.FileTypeFilter.Add("*");
    folderPicker.SettingsIdentifier = "imageFolderPicker";
    folderPicker.SuggestedStartLocation = PickerLocationId.PicturesLibrary;

    var folder = await folderPicker.PickSingleFolderAsync();

    var files = await folder.GetFilesAsync();

    List<ImageGroupItem> items = new List<ImageGroupItem>();
    foreach (StorageFile file in files.Take(6))
{
        BitmapImage photoBitmap = new BitmapImage();
        photoBitmap.SetSource(await file.OpenAsync(FileAccessMode.Read));

    ImageGroupItem item = new ImageGroupItem()
    {
        Image = photoBitmap,
        Title = file.Name,
        Subtitle = file.DateCreated.ToString()
    };
```

```
            items.Add(item);
        }

        gvPhotos.ItemsSource = items;
    }
  }
}
```

Summary

This chapter has introduced WinRT development in .NET. In building the app in this chapter, you have seen several XAML WinRT controls:

- `TextBlock`
- `Button`
- `Image`
- `FilePicker`
- `GridView`
- `FolderPicker`

You have also used data binding and data templating to control the user interface and display of data. These basic approaches to app development apply to nearly all WinRT UI elements.

Hopefully, you are getting excited about WinRT development. If you are already familiar with .NET development, you can see that building apps for Windows 8 is very natural.

In the next chapter, you will learn how to expand your app. You will provide interaction with other apps and see how to access system resources.

CHAPTER 4

Reaching Beyond the App

The world is highly connected. Most likely, the apps you build will need to be connected as well. They might need to connect to an Internet source for data, or they might need to connect to other apps or services on the machine where they are running. This chapter introduces you to concepts involved in extending Metro style apps and connecting with other apps.

This chapter covers:

- Capabilities
- Implementing the Location capability
- Declarations (contracts)
- Implementing the Share declaration (as a source)
- Implementing the Share Target declaration

Capabilities

All Metro style apps are sandboxed. They are isolated from one another and cannot directly access content on the machine where they are running. This provides a secure experience for the user.

However, consumers also expect certain apps to gain access to certain resources on their machine. For example, an app for editing photos would be expected to access the photos on the user's machine. An app that plays videos should be capable of accessing the video library.

This is where *capability declarations* apply. When an app is built that needs to access external resources, those needs must be declared. When an app is installed that has been configured with declarations, the user will be notified what capabilities the app is requesting. This notification is presented prior to installation, giving the user the option to cancel the process if the user prefers not to allow the specific app access to the requested resources.

Note When an app is submitted to the Windows Store, any capability declarations will be checked against the purpose of that app. If the declarations do not appear appropriate for the type of app, it could be rejected.

The Manifest Designer

The capability declarations are predefined by the Windows Runtime. They are configured using the Manifest Designer in Visual Studio. This designer is accessed by opening the **Package.appxmanifest** file in the app project. Figure 4-1 shows how this appears in Visual Studio 11 Beta.

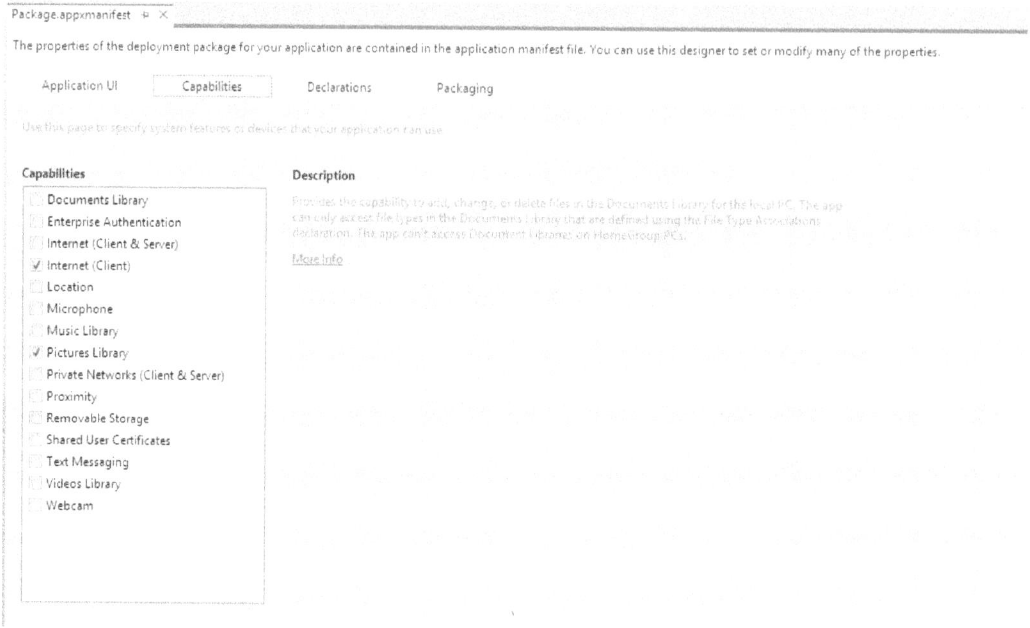

Figure 4-1. Manifest Designer in Visual Studio 11

The capability declarations are managed on the Capabilities tab in the Manifest Designer. This allows for easy manipulation of what is essentially an XML file. Developers simply check the boxes for the appropriate resources their app needs to access.

■ **Note** Capability declarations are only needed if the app desires to access resources *without* the user's explicit permission. If a control such as a `FilePicker` is used to access a picture or video, then that declaration is not necessary. When the user is involved in the process, they are essentially giving permission by choosing the file themselves. Declarations allow apps to programmatically access resources without prompting the user for permission.

The Available Capability Options

WinRT provides access to many types of resources via the following capabilities:

Documents Library: Provides the ability to add, change, or delete files in the Documents Library on the local PC. The types of files the app can access must be declared. This does not grant access to the Document Libraries on other HomeGroup PCs.

Enterprise Authentication: Provides the ability to connect to enterprise resources that require domain credentials.

Internet (Client & Server): Provides inbound and outbound access to the Internet and public networks. The Internet (Client) capability is not needed when this declaration is present.

Internet (Client): Provides outbound access to the Internet and public networks.

Location: Provides access to the current location information available on the PC. This includes cell triangulations, WiFi through IP address, and GPS sensors or devices.

Microphone: Provides access to the microphone's audio feed on the PC.

Music Library: Provides the ability to add, change, or delete files in the user's local Music Library and those on HomeGroup PCs.

Pictures Library: Provides the ability to add, change, or delete files in the user's local Pictures Library and those on HomeGroup PCs.

Private Networks (Client & Server): Provides inbound and outbound access to the home and work networks.

Proximity: Provides the ability to connect to devices in close proximity to the PC using near-field communication. This includes Bluetooth, WiFi, and the Internet.

Removable Storage: Provides the ability to add, change, or delete files on any removable storage devices connected to the PC. The types of files the app can access must be declared. This does not grant access to removable storage devices on HomeGroup PCs.

Shared User Certificates: Provides the ability to access software and hardware certificates, including smart card certificates.

Text Messaging: Provides access to the SMS functionality on the PC. This includes onboard cellular chips that can be present in tablets, or connected cell phones and data devices in laptops.

Videos Library: Provides the ability to add, change, or delete files in the user's local Videos Library and those on HomeGroup PCs.

Webcam: Provides access to the webcam's video feed on the PC.

■ **Note** The Documents Library and Removable Storage capabilities require File Type Associations declarations to filter which types of files to grant access. These declarations will be discussed in more detail later in this chapter.

Implement the Location Capability

Visual Studio provides a straightforward process for configuring an app's capabilities. This removes the difficulty of implementation, leaving the developer to concentrate on the app's design and the proper use of the resources available. In this section, you will build a simple app that uses location information via the Location capability.

Create the Solution

You will begin with a Visual C# Blank Application template and add a simple UI to display the current location of the PC using the WiFi connection.

1. Start Visual Studio 11 and select the Blank Application template in the Visual C# Windows Metro style section. Name the solution **WinRT_Location** and select the appropriate location on your PC. When your screen appears similar to Figure 4-2, click OK.

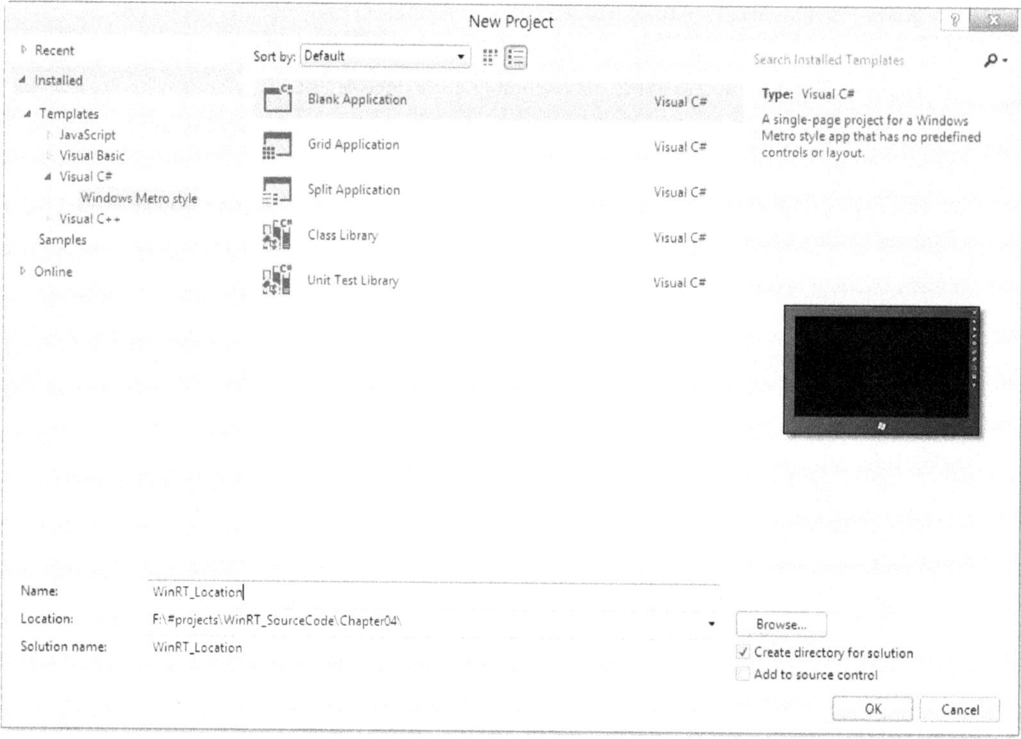

Figure 4-2. *Creating the WinRT_Location project*

2. Open the **Package.appxmanifest** file. This will bring up the Manifest Designer. Click the Capabilities tab and select the Location option, as shown in Figure 4-3.

Figure 4-3. *Selecting the Location capability*

3. Open **BlankPage.xaml**. Replace the empty grid with the following code:

```
<Grid Background="Silver">
      <Grid.RowDefinitions>
          <RowDefinition Height="80" />
          <RowDefinition Height="300" />
          <RowDefinition Height="100"/>
          <RowDefinition />
      </Grid.RowDefinitions>
      <TextBlock Grid.Row="0" FontSize="36" TextAlignment="Center"
       Margin="20">Find My Location</TextBlock>
      <Border Grid.Row="1" BorderBrush="Black" BorderThickness="2">
        <TextBlock x:Name="lblLocation" Grid.Row="1" FontSize="24"
         TextAlignment="Center" Width="800" Margin="20"></TextBlock>
      </Border>
      <Button x:Name="btnFindLocation" Grid.Row="2"
       Content="Where Am I" HorizontalAlignment="Center"
       Click="btnFindLocation_Click_1"></Button>
    </Grid>
```

This XAML code describes a simple grid of a title, a TextBlock control for display, and a Button control. When the button is clicked, the app will display the current location information in the TextBlock control. A Border control is used to indicate the location of the empty TextBlock before the user clicks the button.

4. Open **BlankPage.xaml.cs**. Add the following namespace to gain access to the WinRT components involved in geolocation:

```
using Windows.Devices.Geolocation;
```

5. Add the following method to handle the button click event:

```
async private void btnFindLocation_Click_1(object sender,
   RoutedEventArgs e)
{
   var locator = new Geolocator();
      locator.DesiredAccuracy = PositionAccuracy.Default;

      var position = await locator.GetGeopositionAsync();
      this.LoadPosition(position);
}
```

WinRT has made getting the current location extremely simple and straightforward. The Geolocator.GetGeopositionAsync() method uses the existing location resources and returns the current geolocation information as a Geoposition object.

Just prior to calling the GetGeopositionAsync() method, the DesiredAccuracy property is set. There are two values for this property, Default and High. The Default setting is optimized for power and performance. The High setting will produce more accurate results, but it will also use more battery power and connection bandwidth. The High setting should be reserved to only those situations where accuracy is absolutely necessary, or power and performance are not a factor.

6. Add the following method to display the information found in the returned `Geoposition` object:

```
private void LoadPosition(Geoposition position)
  {
      string locationText = "";

      locationText = "You have been located!" + Environment.NewLine;
      locationText += Environment.NewLine;
      locationText += "Your coordinates are " +
        position.Coordinate.Longitude + " longitude and " +
        position.Coordinate.Latitude + " latitude " + Environment.NewLine;
      locationText += Environment.NewLine;

      if (string.IsNullOrWhiteSpace(position.CivicAddress.City))
      {
          locationText += "Your local address information is not
            available at this time" + Environment.NewLine;
          locationText += Environment.NewLine;
      }
      else
      {
          locationText += "You may recognize this location as " +
            position.CivicAddress.City + ", " + position.CivicAddress.State + " " +
            position.CivicAddress.PostalCode + Environment.NewLine;
          locationText += Environment.NewLine;
      }

      locationText += "It is currently " +
          position.CivicAddress.Timestamp.DateTime.ToString() + " at your location";

      lblLocation.Text = locationText;
  }
```

This text builds a string for display from the information found in the `Geoposition` object returned by the Windows Runtime. The longitude and latitude information is available in the `Coordinate` property. Local information, such as `City`, `State`, `Postal Code`, and the local time stored in a property named `TimeStamp`, is available through the `CivicAddress` property.

Run the Location App

Now the app is ready to test.

1. Press F5 to run the app. Click the button and your screen should appear similar to Figure 4-4.

Perhaps you were not expecting to get a prompt for permission since the app included the capability declaration. Location is one of the items that Windows protects with an extra layer of certainty by prompting the user the *first time* the resource is accessed by the app. Once the user has made their choice, the app will not prompt again.

■ **Note** While WinRT components essentially access the Windows Core directly, there is a layer of security within this process. The broker service ensures that Metro style apps only access the resources for which they have permission.

Figure 4-4. *Permission request for location information*

2. Click **Allow** to provide permission to the location information. Your screen should now appear similar to Figure 4-5.

■ **Note** Depending on your hardware configuration, you may experience different results. The project for this book was run on a laptop, and the location information was obtained through the WiFi connection. The `CivicAddress` property was not fully populated.

The same approach would be used to implement the capabilities in an app. The option must be checked within the **Package.appxmanifest** file before the app is granted access.

Figure 4-5. *WinRT_Location running successfully*

Declarations (Contracts)

When WinRT was described at the 2011 Build conference, the word "contract" was used to describe how Windows Runtime components gained exposure to other components on the system. This is a good conceptual word.

However, in the Visual Studio 11 Manifest Designer, these contracts are called *declarations*. They will also be referred to as declarations for the remainder of this chapter.

Declaration Options

The Windows Runtime provides many declaration options. These options are found in the **Package.appxmanifest** file under the Declarations tab, as shown in Figure 4-6.

This list contains the following options:

> *Account Picture Provider:* Provides the context for an app to allow a user to change their account picture.
>
> *AutoPlay Content:* Provides the context for configuring an app to launch when specific content types are detected.
>
> *AutoPlay Device:* Provides the context for configuring an app to launch when specific devices are detected.
>
> *Background Tasks:* Provides the context to run tasks while an app is suspended.
>
> *Cached File Updater:* Provides the context for an app to update specific files to ensure they are tracked and maintained.
>
> *Camera Settings:* Provides the context to expose camera options to the user.
>
> *Certificates:* Provides the context to install digital certificates for authentication, typically over SSL.
>
> *Contact Picker:* Provides the context to gain access to contact data.

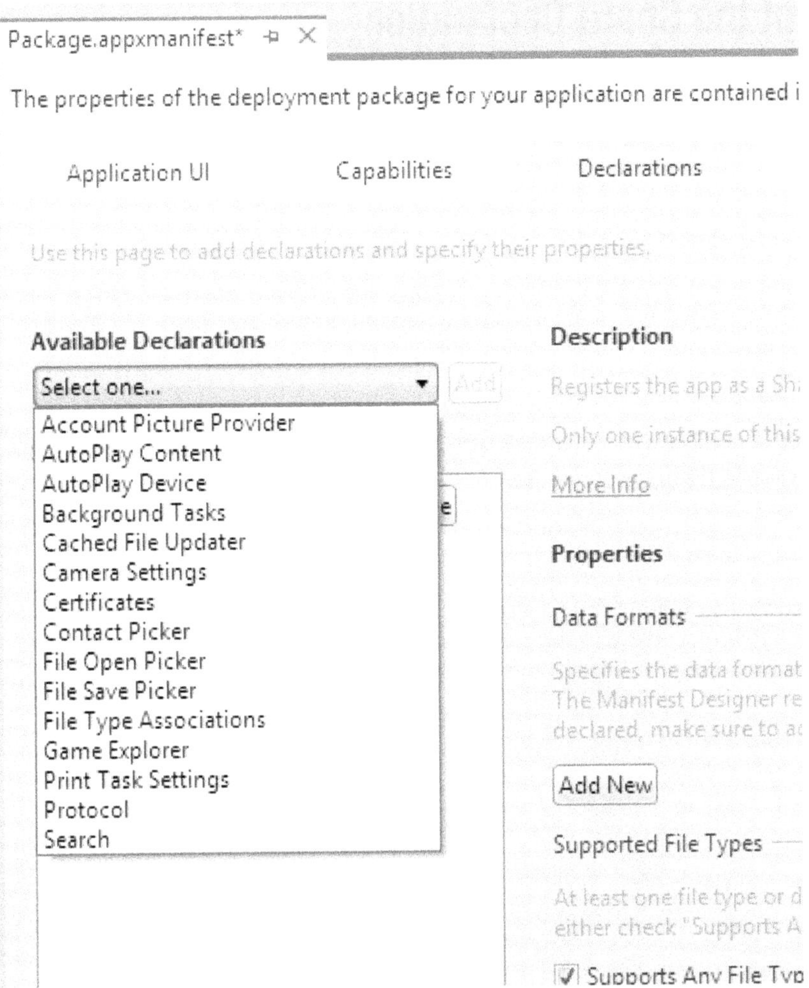

***Figure 4-6.** WinRT declaration options*

File Open Picker: Provides the context for apps to find and open files from other apps.

File Save Picker: Provides the context for saving files on the system.

File Type Associations: Provides the context to gain access to certain file types. If a file type is not declared, the app will not be allowed access without explicit permission from the user.

Game Explorer: Provides the context to register with Windows as a game.

Print Task Settings: Provides the context for a custom user interface for accessing print devices.

Protocol: Provides the context to use existing protocols as well as create custom ones.

Search: Provides the context for searching within the app or searching within other apps. This declaration will provide access for searching by other apps as well.

Implement the Share Declaration

Sharing is an important feature for an app. Many users expect information to be shareable within many apps. Even simple games are expected to share scoring information and such.

In this section, you will build a simple app that shares text information. This app will serve as the source in the sharing activity.

Create the Solution

In this section you will build a Visual C# Metro style app using the Blank Application template and add a simple UI to write some text. You will then add the ability to respond to the Share Charm as well as provide button to initial the sharing experience.

■ **Note** Windows 8 provides a new UI feature called Charms. They appear on the right side of the Start screen and are universally available. Users can access them from within any app. The Charms available are Search, Share, Start, Devices and Settings.

---

1. Open Visual Studio 11 and select the Blank Application template in the Visual C# Metro style section. Name the project **WinRT_Sharing** and choose the appropriate location on your PC. When your screen looks similar to Figure 4-7, click OK.

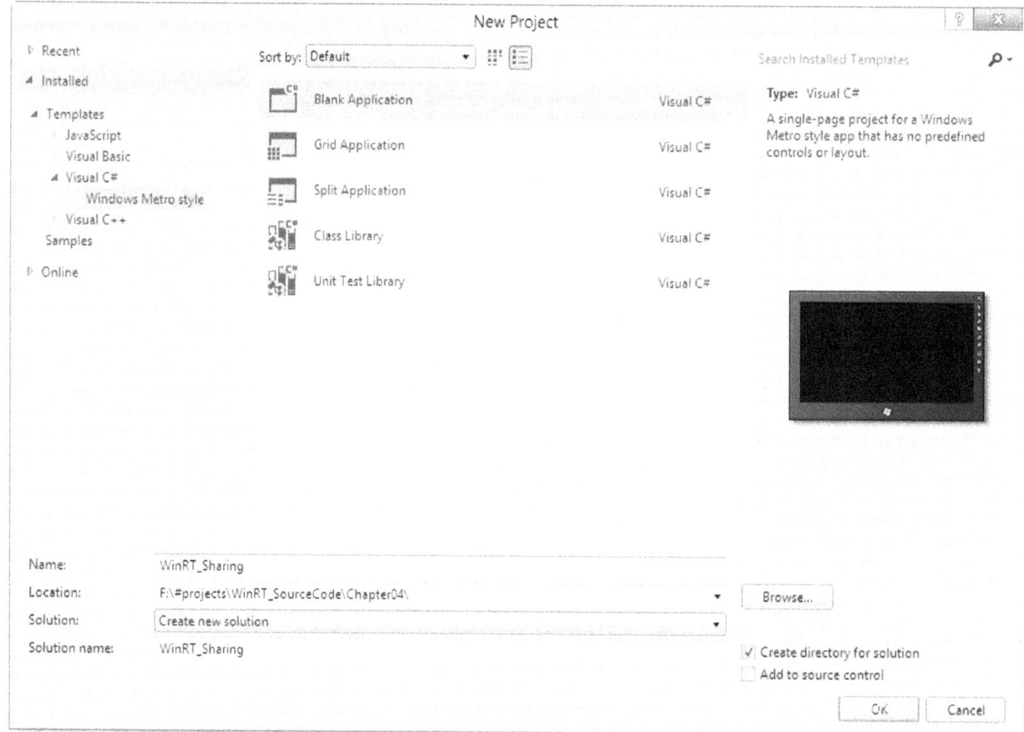

***Figure 4-7.** Creating the WinRT_Sharing project*

2. Open **BlankPage.xaml** and replace the empty grid with the following code:

```
<Grid Background="Silver">
    <Grid.RowDefinitions>
        <RowDefinition Height="30" />
        <RowDefinition Height="220" />
        <RowDefinition Height="50" />
        <RowDefinition />
    </Grid.RowDefinitions>
    <TextBlock Grid.Row="0" FontSize="18" TextAlignment="Center"
     VerticalAlignment="Center">Text to Share</TextBlock>
    <TextBox x:Name="txtPostText" Grid.Row="1" Height="150" Width="500"
     TextWrapping="Wrap" Margin="10"></TextBox>
    <Button x:Name="btnPost" Grid.Row="2" Content="Share"
     HorizontalAlignment="Center" Click="btnPost_Click_1"></Button>
    <StackPanel Grid.Row="3">
      <Button x:Name="btnFindContact" Content="Pick a contact"
       HorizontalAlignment="Center" Margin="20" Click="btnFindContact_Click_1"></
       Button>
      <TextBlock x:Name="lblContact"
       HorizontalAlignment="Center"></TextBlock>
      </StackPanel>
</Grid>
```

This markup code adds a title, a TextBox control for typing, and a Button control. The designer in Visual Studio should appear similar to Figure 4-8.

Figure 4-8. *WinRT_Sharing UI in the designer*

3. Open **BlankPage.xaml.cs**. Add the following namespace to gain access to the sharing functionality in WinRT:

```
using Windows.ApplicationModel.DataTransfer;
```

4. Add the following code to handle the event when data is requested from this app:

```
DataTransferManager.GetForCurrentView().DataRequested +=
   BlankPage_DataRequested;
```

5. Add the following method to handle the data request event:

```
void BlankPage_DataRequested(DataTransferManager sender,
   DataRequestedEventArgs args)
```

```
{
    args.Request.Data.Properties.Title = "Test Post";
    args.Request.Data.Properties.Description = "Testing sharing from Windows 8";
    args.Request.Data.SetText(txtPostText.Text);
}
```

The BlankPage_DataRequested() method is called when Windows 8 requests data from the app through the sharing process. The Sharing Charm is accessible to the users while the app is running; users can request to share information at almost any time.

This method declares the Title and Description properties for display and then calls the SetText() property. This ensures that only text is being shared from this app. Only apps that are configured to receive text will appear in the Share UI.

6. Add the following method to handle the button click:

```
private void btnPost_Click_1(object sender, RoutedEventArgs e)
  {
     DataTransferManager.ShowShareUI();
  }
```

The code within this method displays the Share UI. The user can then initiate the sharing experience directly from within the app rather than from the Charms UI.

Run the Sharing App

Now the app is ready to test.

1. Press F5 to run the app. Enter some text into the TextBox control. Your screen should appear similar to Figure 4-9.

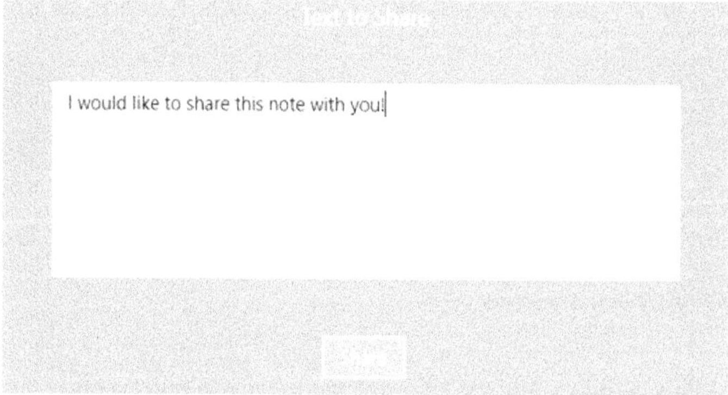

Figure 4-9. *WinRT_Sharing running successfully*

2. Either access the Charms and click the Share Charm, or click the **Share** button within the app to initiate sharing. Your screen should appear similar to Figure 4-10.

■ **Note** The list of apps in the Share UI may appear different on your machine, depending on what apps are installed. At the time of writing this app, only the Mail app was configured to receive text through the Share UI.

Figure 4-10. Sharing from WinRT_Sharing

3. Choose the Mail app. This will bring up the specific UI presented by the Mail app for receiving text. That UI appears as shown in Figure 4-11.

Figure 4-11. Sharing text through the Mail app Share UI

You should notice that a specific declaration was not necessary to allow this app to engage in sharing. The app did implement the concept of the sharing contract, but to push information, the Windows system does not require declarations to exist.

This is not the case when accepting information through sharing, as will be demonstrated in the next section.

Implement the Share Target Declaration

In this section you will build a Visual C# app to accept a photo through the Share UI. You will configure the UI to present for accepting the photo.

Create the Solution

You will first build a project using the Blank Application template for Visual C# Metro style apps. You will then design the UI to present when accepting shared information and configure the app to respond when photo information is being shared.

1. Open Visual Studio 11 and create a new project using the Visual C# Windows Metro style Blank Application template. Name the project **WinRT_ShareTarget** and choose the appropriate location on your PC. When your screen appears similar to Figure 4-12, click OK.

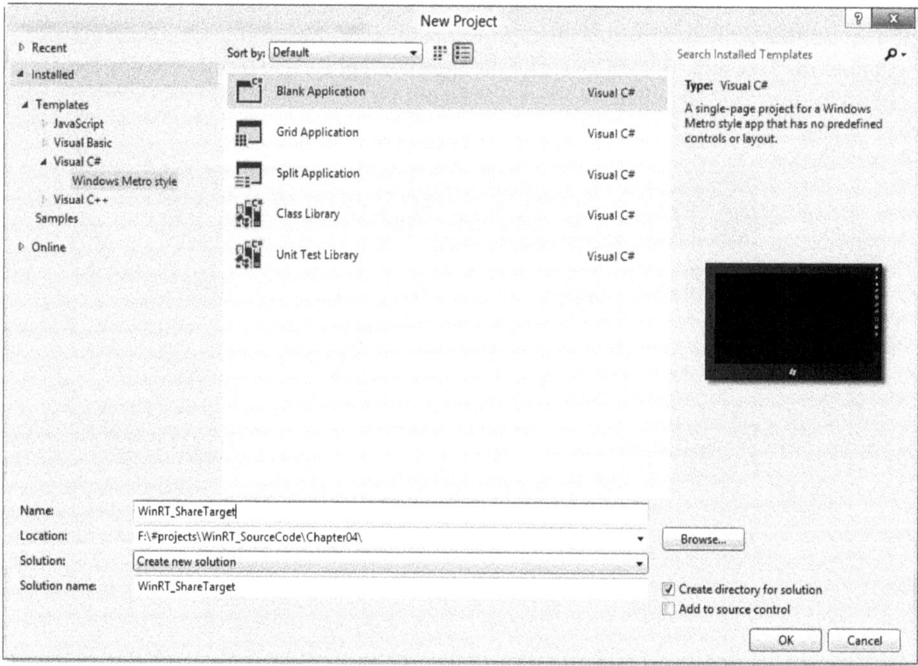

Figure 4-12. *Creating the WinRT_ShareTarget project*

2. Right-click the solution and click Add New Item. Choose a BlankPage and name it **ShareTarget.xaml**.

3. Open **ShareTarget.xaml** and replace the empty grid with the following code:

```
<Grid Background="{StaticResource ApplicationPageBackgroundBrush}">
    <Grid.RowDefinitions>
        <RowDefinition Height="75" />
        <RowDefinition />
        <RowDefinition />
```

```
        </Grid.RowDefinitions>
        <StackPanel Background="silver" Grid.Row="0">
            <TextBlock FontSize="36">WinRT Sharing</TextBlock>
        </StackPanel>

        <StackPanel Orientation="Vertical" Grid.Row="1">
            <Image x:Name="imgShare" Width="400"></Image>
            <TextBlock x:Name="lblMessage"></TextBlock>
        </StackPanel>
        <Button x:Name="btnShare" Content="Share" Grid.Row="2"
         HorizontalAlignment="Center" Click="btnShare_Click_1"></Button>
    </Grid>
```

This markup code creates a simple UI with a title, an area to display an image, and a button. This will serve as the UI presented when this app is selected to share a photo. That is done in a slim window on the right of the screen, so the page width needs to change.

4. Add the following attribute to the Page element in **ShareTarget.xaml**:

```
Width="600"
```

The designer in Visual Studio should look similar to Figure 4-13.

Figure 4-13. *ShareTarget.xaml in the Visual Studio designer*

5. Open **Package.appxmanifest**. Click the Declarations tab.

6. In the Available Declarations drop-down list, select Share Target. Click the **Add** button.

7. Under the Data Formats section on the right side of the screen, click the **Add New** button and enter **Bitmap** as the data format.

Your screen should appear as shown in Figure 4-14.

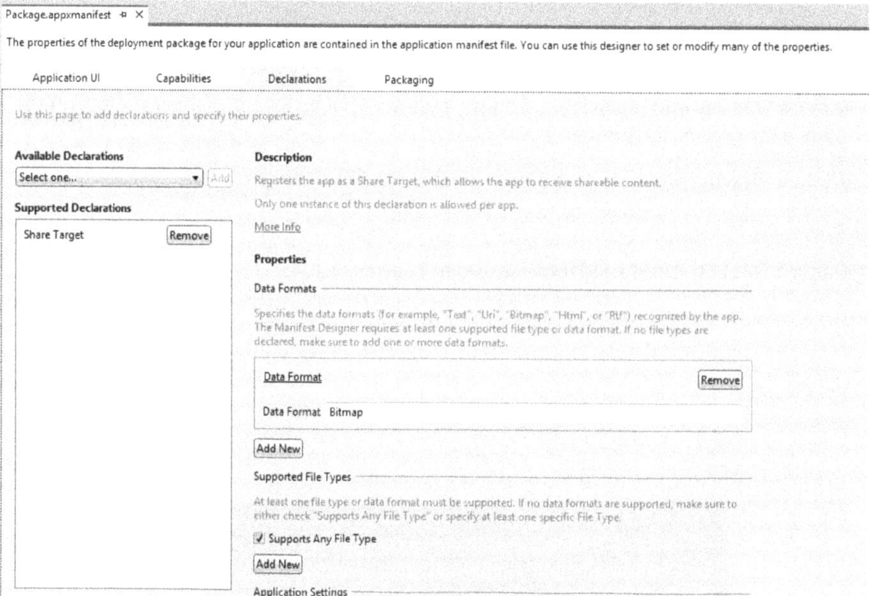

Figure 4-14. *WinRT_ShareTarget declarations*

These changes ensure that the app is configured to respond to the sharing event when the type of data being shared is a `Bitmap`.

When a sharing event occurs, Windows presents a list of apps that have declared they accept the type of data being shared. Another event is triggered when the user selects an app.

8. Open **App.xaml.cs**. Add the following method to handle the event when the app is selected as the Share Target:

```
protected override void OnShareTargetActivated(
    ShareTargetActivatedEventArgs args)
  {
      var shareTarget = new ShareTarget();
      shareTarget.Activate(args);
      Window.Current.Content = shareTarget;
      Window.Current.Activate();
  }
```

This code instantiates the ShareTarget page and calls the Activate() method, passing in the ShareTargetActivatedEventArgs. This essentially allows the page to set up using the information about the share request, including the data being shared.

Once the Activate() method completes, the ShareTarget page is displayed to the user to complete the share experience.

Now the ShareTarget page must be coded to handle this request.

9. Open **ShareTarget.xaml.cs**. Add the following namespaces:

```
using Windows.ApplicationModel.Activation;
using Windows.UI.Xaml.Media.Imaging;
using Windows.ApplicationModel.DataTransfer.ShareTarget;
using Windows.ApplicationModel.DataTransfer;
using Windows.Storage.Streams;
using Windows.Storage;
```

10. Add the following code to implement the Activate() method:

```
public void Activate(ShareTargetActivatedEventArgs args)
  {
      if (args.Kind != ActivationKind.ShareTarget) return;

      this.LoadShareTextAsync(args);

      _shareOperation = args.ShareOperation;
  }
```

This method checks the arguments passed in to ensure that only ShareTarget events are handled. Then a private method is called to process the parameters, and the ShareOperation object is stored into a private member for use later.

11. Add the following code to implement the LoadShareTextAsync() method:

```
async private void LoadShareTextAsync(
    ShareTargetActivatedEventArgs args)
  {
      if (args.ShareOperation.Data.Contains(
        StandardDataFormats.Bitmap))
      {

        var imageStreamRef = await
          args.ShareOperation.Data.GetBitmapAsync();
        var imageStream = await imageStreamRef.OpenReadAsync();
        BitmapImage bitmap = new BitmapImage();
        bitmap.SetSource(imageStream);
        imgShare.Source = bitmap;

        lblMessage.Text = "image loaded";
      }
      else if (args.ShareOperation.Data.Contains(
        StandardDataFormats.StorageItems))
      {
        var files = await
          args.ShareOperation.Data.GetStorageItemsAsync();
        var file = (StorageFile)files[0];
```

```
            BitmapImage bitmap = new BitmapImage();
            bitmap.SetSource(await file.OpenAsync(
              Windows.Storage.FileAccessMode.Read)
        );
              imgShare.Source = bitmap;
        }
    }
```

First, notice the async keyword is used in the method declaration. Since at least one asynchronous method will be called within this method, the async keyword is required.

This method handles two scenarios: one when the shared information is in the Bitmap format, and the other when the shared information is in the StorageItems format. This app is designed to accept photos. This type of data may be shared as either one of these formats.

If the data is of type Bitmap, the GetBitmapAsyc() method is used. This returns a reference to a stream. The OpenReadAsync() method is called to return the actual stream. From there, a BitmapImage may be created and set as the source of the Image control on the page.

If the data is of type StoredImages, the GetStorageItemsAsync() method is called to get a list of files that are being shared. This app is written to only accept one image, so only the first file of this list is referenced. Again, a BitmapImage is created and used to set the source of the Image control.

Note Along with the async keyword used in the method declaration, the await keyword is also used within this method. As discussed in previous chapters, the await keyword is the simple syntax for handling asynchronous method calls in C#.

---

12. Add the following method to handle the button click event:

```
private void btnShare_Click_1(object sender, RoutedEventArgs e)
  {
      _shareOperation.ReportCompleted();
      _shareOperation = null;
  }
```

This app simply reports back to the initiating app that the share operation is complete. In a typical app, this event would handle the data and store it or present it within the app. This demonstration simply walks through the share experience itself.

Note Buildinga full app to accept and handle the data being shared is beyond the scope of this chapter. How that is handled depends on the purpose of the app itself. The data could simply be displayed onto a separate page, or the file could be stored somewhere on the system. It could possibly be passed along to an online service. The options for handling the shared data are endless.

Run the Share Target App

This app is written to respond to the sharing events. Typically, an entire UI would be written and this sharing page would only provide a minor role. As it is, there is no real UI for this app. Rather than running the app for testing, you will need to deploy the app and initiate a sharing experience for this app to respond.

1. Right-click the solution and click Deploy, as shown in Figure 4-15.

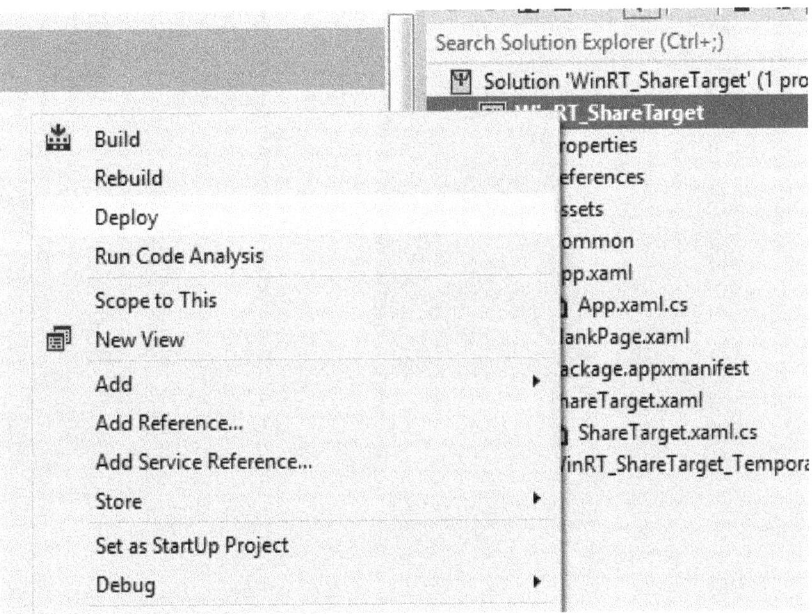

Figure 4-15. *Deploying the WinRT_ShareTarget app*

2. Navigate to the Windows 8 Start screen and select the Photo app.
3. Browse the available photos and select one. Figure 4-16 shows a selected photo in the Photo app.

■ **Note** On a laptop, photos are selected by right-clicking them. For hardware with a touch interface, the experience will be different.

Figure 4-16. *Selected photo in the Photo app*

4. Access the Windows 8 Charms. Figure 4-17 shows the Windows 8 Charms.
5. Click the Share Charm. This will display the apps available to accept a photo through sharing. Notice that WinRT_ShareTarget is listed among the available apps. You should see something similar to Figure 4-18.
6. Click the WinRT_ShareTarget app in the Share list. This should present the UI, as shown in Figure 4-19.
7. Click the **Share** button. The share experience should end and you should be taken back to the Photo app.

Figure 4-17. *The Windows 8 Charms*

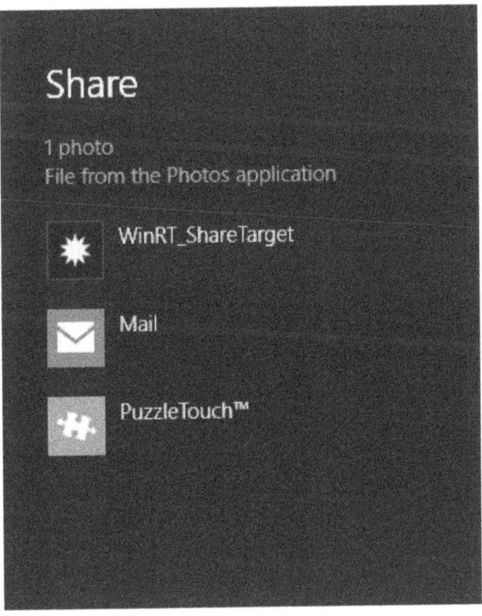

Figure 4-18. *WinRT_ShareTarget listed as a target app for sharing photos*

Figure 4-19. *Share UI from WinRT_ShareTarget*

Summary

Building sandboxed apps is important for a secure and controlled experience for users. However, those same users desire connectivity, and they expect it from their apps. The Windows Runtime provides the infrastructure to develop safe and secure interconnected apps. You have been introduced to the concepts that make this happen:

- Capabilities
- Declarations

You have implemented these concepts into working apps. You used the Location capability to find the geolocation of the device running your app.

You have implemented the sharing contract, both as a source and by using the Share Target declaration. You have seen how apps can respond to system events and handle shared information.

This book has introduced you to the Windows Runtime in Windows 8. The fundamentals demonstrated within this book provide the foundation for app building in the Windows 8 ecosystem.

Take these sample projects and extend their functionality. Space was limited in this book, so only a few examples were included.

The Appendix includes references to resources for further investigation and exposure to the Windows Runtime. Some resources expound on topics within this book. Some address topics this book could not cover.

I hope you have found this book helpful. WinRT is a new and exciting opportunity for developers. This book has attempted to answer some of the questions you may have about WinRT and, through the knowledge presented, enhance your ability to build Windows 8 apps.

APPENDIX

WinRT Resources

This appendix contains resources that you may find helpful as you explore WinRT in more depth. Many of them were used during the research of this book, so they should help to expound on the topics covered. Some of them address topics that were not covered in this book; WinRT is a big subject, and this book simply introduced it.

Channel 9 on MSDN

Channel 9 has many resources for developers concerning WinRT. Visit the main site at `http://channel9.msdn.com` and search for "windows runtime" for a list.

Recommended Videos from Channel 9

- Using the Windows Runtime from C# and Visual Basic

  `http://channel9.msdn.com/Events/BUILD/BUILD2011/TOOL-531T`

- Lap around the Windows Runtime

  `http://channel9.msdn.com/Events/BUILD/BUILD2011/PLAT-874T`

2011 Build Conference Web Site

The 2011 Build conference is a little dated, but the information found on its site—`www.buildwindows.com`—is still helpful regarding WinRT.

Windows Dev Center

One of the primary resources is the Windows Dev Center (`http://dev.windows.com`). This is the starting place for Microsoft's documentation regarding Windows 8 development and WinRT. Here are a few links to start with, but the Windows Dev Center is a vast collection of information. It will serve as a point of reference you will return to time and again.

- Learn to build Metro style apps

  `http://msdn.microsoft.com/library/windows/apps`

- API reference for Metro style apps

  `http://msdn.microsoft.com/en-us/library/windows/apps/br211369.aspx`

- API reference for Windows Runtime and Windows Library for JavaScript

  http://msdn.microsoft.com/en-us/library/windows/apps/br211377.aspx

- Metro style app fundamentals

  http://msdn.microsoft.com/en-us/library/windows/apps/hh750302.aspx

- App capability declarations

  http://msdn.microsoft.com/en-us/library/windows/apps/hh464936.aspx

- App contracts and extensions

  http://msdn.microsoft.com/en-us/library/windows/apps/hh464906.aspx

Miguel de Icaza: "WinRT Demystified"

Miguel de Icaza wrote a nice article regarding WinRT.

- "WinRT Demystified"

  http://tirania.org/blog/archive/2011/Sep-15.html

WinRT on CodePlex

CodePlex has a spot of WinRT utilities and related development projects.

- CodePlex WinRT

  http://winrt.codeplex.com

Doug Steven: "A Bad Picture Is Worth a Thousand Long Discussions"

Doug Steven discusses the Windows Runtime architecture diagram and what is missing.

- "A Bad Picture Is Worth a Thousand Long Discussions"

  http://dougseven.com/2011/09/15/a-bad-picture-is-worth-a-thousand-long-discussions

DevHawk: "The Windows Runtime"

This article is from a blog written by a developer on the WinRT team.

- "The Windows Runtime"

  http://devhawk.net/2011/09/15/the-windows-runtime

Index

A, B

C, D, E

F

G, H, I

J, K

L

M

N

O, P, Q, R

S

T

U

V

W, X, Y, Z

GPSR Compliance
The European Union's (EU) General Product Safety Regulation (GPSR) is a set of rules that requires consumer products to be safe and our obligations to ensure this.

If you have any concerns about our products, you can contact us on

ProductSafety@springernature.com

In case Publisher is established outside the EU, the EU authorized representative is:

Springer Nature Customer Service Center GmbH
Europaplatz 3
69115 Heidelberg, Germany

www.ingramcontent.com/pod-product-compliance
Ingram Content Group UK Ltd.
Pitfield, Milton Keynes, MK11 3LW, UK
UKHW051838231225
466357UK00013B/236

9781430245841